FAVORITE BIBLE PASSAGES

VOLUME 1
REVISED EDITION

BRADY B. WHITEHEAD, JR.
&
HOWARD H. HAM

ABINGDON PRESS
Nashville

FAVORITE BIBLE PASSAGES
Volume 1
Revised Edition

Copyright © 1989 by Graded Press.
Revised Edition Copyright © 1998 by Abingdon Press.

ISBN 13: 978-0-687-07199-9

This book is printed on acid-free paper.

MANUFACTURED IN THE UNITED STATES OF AMERICA.

07 08 09 10 11 12–18 17 16 15 14 13 12

CONTENTS

"ONE OF MY FAVORITES!"

Whether we are talking about a menu item at the dinner table or a song on the radio, how good it feels to recognize a favorite. But sometimes the word *favorite* causes uncomfortable feelings.

"Play favorites" is an expression that suggests an unfair choice. "Isaac preferred Esau. . . . . but Rebecca preferred Jacob" (Genesis 25:28, *Good News Bible: The Bible in Today's English Version* [TEV]) is a glimpse of biblical parenthood that points to trouble ahead. "Favoritism" is a pattern of human relationships that hinders personal growth and the ability to receive God's love.

Why, then, do we publish a study book called *Favorite Bible Passages*? Is any reader likely to glance at the contents and say, "Yes, these are the twenty-six passages I like best in all the Bible"?

Probably not. Some readers may say, "They left out one of my favorites."

These twenty-six passages are certainly not the only well-loved parts of Scripture. They are a few of the Bible texts that have stood the test of time, that people have turned to for fresh insights and divine guidance generation after generation.

We trust that each of the selections will communicate God's love and guidance to you and to others among our readers.

We are convinced that God can and does speak to persons through the Bible. We pray that this volume will help our readers hear God's message more clearly.

The Editors
FAVORITE BIBLE PASSAGES

1
IT WAS GOOD

Genesis 1:1–2:4a

God saw everything that he had made, and indeed, it was very good.

Genesis 1:31

WORDS FOR BIBLE TIMES

"In the beginning when God created the heavens and the earth" (Genesis 1:1). What a magnificent opening line for the Holy Scriptures! The Bible seems to be saying, "Let there be no mistake. The God who ministers to our needs, comforts us in our sorrows, and guides us in our daily living is the same God who created the entire universe." That thought is awesome, almost unbelievable. Yet there it is, on the very first page of the Bible. What wonderful words of assurance these are!

However, not everyone puts the same value on these words. Some people smile indulgently when they read this account of Creation. They think of it as a simple, childlike explanation coming from a primitive and unsophisticated people. However, these persons are wrong. To be sure, the Bible gives us a prescientific version of how the world came into existence. Nevertheless, the biblical account of Creation is well thought out, highly structured, and designed to combat the theologically anemic stories of Creation that were current at the time it was written.

In virtually all the Creation stories of Israel's neighbors, the earth was brought into being through conflict and rivalry. In the influential Babylonian version, for example, the conquering god made the earth by splitting the body of his rival in two. He formed the earth with one half of her body and the sky with the other. In contrast, the Book of Genesis mentions only one God; and this God creates without conflict and without effort. God speaks a word, and it is done.

Move now to Genesis 1:14. Israel's neighbors thought of the sun, the moon, and the stars as gods. These gods supposedly controlled the destinies of human beings, and each god tried to outdo the others for control of the whole earth. In the Book of Genesis, however, the "lights in the dome of the sky" are not gods at all. The one true God created them, and they are under the control of their Creator. They serve the purposes for which God created them—to give light and to mark off the seasons, the days, and the years. The Bible does not call the sun and the moon by name. Their very names were synonymous with the pagan gods.

(1) Presence of God.
(2) shows everything
(3) truth way

The Book of Genesis, then, does not give us a childish description of Creation. This account of Creation is a solid piece of theological writing, written in a poetic style. It tells us—far better than a prosaic paragraph or two ever could—that our God is the only God there is and that all things are under our God's control.

WORDS FOR OUR TIME

Suppose for a moment that you are quite skilled at making things. Perhaps you knit sweaters. Maybe you build furniture or compose music or paint. Whatever it is that you do, pretend now that you have done it. Suppose further that the work you have just completed is the best piece that you have ever done. With great pride you give it to the person whom you love the most. Now suppose that after some time has passed, you look again at the work you gave to your loved one. But alas—it no longer looks like the fine work of art you created. Instead, it is stained and ugly. It is chipped and broken. Large pieces have been torn off. It has been neglected, soiled, and abused. How do you feel about that? Are you sorry you ever gave it to him or her?

Now let your mind go back to the biblical account of Creation. Six times in the first chapter of Genesis we are told that God looked at what he had made and pronounced it "good"—*six times* (verses 4, 10, 12, 18, 21, and 25). In other words, the Creator was quite pleased with what he had created. Creation turned out just as God intended. Then God entrusted that creation to the crown of all creation—human beings. And what happened? We abused it, defaced it, squandered it, exploited it, and poisoned it, caring little if we ruined its beauty and its usefulness to future generations as long as we got "ours." How must that make God feel?

We know that God is a forgiving God. We are familiar with the fact that "God so loved the world that he gave his only Son, so that everyone who believes in him may not perish but may have eternal life" (John 3:16). But does that love include the physical world as well as the people who live in it? Does God want the physical earth to be restored? Will God forgive our foolishness in poisoning the earth and give it new life? This was the prophetic hope (Ezekiel 47:1-12), Paul's hope (Romans 8:21-23), and John the seer's hope (Revelation 22:1-5). This hope is ours as well. But what is our responsibility in helping that hope become reality? How can we restore the earth in order that we might then protect the earth and be good stewards of it?

WORDS FOR MY LIFE

What does it mean to say that you and I are created in the "image" and "likeness" of God (Genesis 1:26)? Many answers have been given to that question. Usually the question is answered on the basis of characteristics that distinguish us from the lower animals, such as superior intelligence, self-consciousness and God-consciousness, the ability to communicate with God, a sense of awe and wonder, the capacity for religion, a sense of the spiritual and of right and wrong, the freedom to choose, and the power to make things. The author of Genesis 1 may have had one or more of these qualities in mind when he spoke of our being in the image of God. But another possibility exists.

The Hebrew word we translate as "image" means a representation. The image represented something or someone else. Thus, the word was used of an idol (2 Kings 11:18; Amos 5:26) or of a statue of a king (Daniel 3:1). Indeed, the king of a vast empire often had images of himself placed at various locations in the empire. He could not visit every portion of his kingdom, but his image reminded the people of his rule. Perhaps it is in that sense that we are in God's image. We are God's representatives on earth.

However, if that interpretation is correct, notice what that does to God's injunction to us to "have dominion . . . over all the wild animals of the earth" (Genesis 1:26). If we represent God, then we are to rule over the fish, the birds, the cattle, and the earth in the same way that God does. God pronounced the created order "very good." We as God's representatives are to preserve that goodness. We are to respect and protect the beauty and orderliness of the world. I believe that is what it means to be in God's image.

Notice one other thing. God did not create human beings and later make them in his image. Rather, God created a being whose very essence was in God's likeness. When we refuse to be like God, we are denying the very purpose of our being. We become more like the animals than like the "male and female" created in God's own image. Could that be why the seventh day of Creation, a day of rest, ultimately became a day of worship? Do we need that day of worship to keep in touch with the reality of who we are? God apparently thought so.

2
GOD'S PROMISE TO ABRAM

Genesis 12

The LORD said to Abram, "Go from your country and your kindred and your father's house to the land that I will show you. I will make of you a great nation, and I will bless you, and make your name great, so that you will be a blessing."

Genesis 12:1-2

WORDS FOR BIBLE TIMES

Of all the hymns ever written, "Amazing Grace" has one of the best titles. God's grace is truly amazing.

God demonstrated this grace from the very beginning. God created Adam and Eve and put them in the garden of Eden. Surely they could have wanted nothing more than that! But the one thing God forbade them do, they did. So the Almighty punished them, requiring that they leave Eden. However, before they left, God made for them "garments of skins...and clothed them" (Genesis 3:21), an expression of God's continuing love.

Then there was Cain. Cain's murder of his brother Abel was so heinous that God made him "a fugitive and a wanderer on the earth" (Genesis 4:12). But God did not send Cain off defenseless. God put a protective mark on him, "so that no one who came upon him would kill him" (Genesis 4:15). Things eventually got so bad that God had to flood the earth to rid it of wickedness. But again, in grace God blessed the survivors of the Flood (Genesis 9:1). When human sin reared its ugly head once more, God scattered the people "over the face of all the earth" and confused their language in what looked like a final, determined effort to rid the world of sin (Genesis 11:8-9). Yet even after that, God came again in his grace, this time to a man named Abram (later known as Abraham; see Genesis 17:1-5).

"Now the LORD said to Abram, 'Go from your country and your kindred and your father's house to the land that I will show you. I will make of you a great nation, and I will bless you, and make your name great, so that you will be a blessing' " (Genesis 12:1-2). Then we read, "So Abram went, as the LORD had told him" (Genesis 12:4).

The obedience of Abram to this call is almost as startling as the call itself. We see not the slightest hint of hesitation on Abram's part. God called; and Abram went, just like that. True, God offered him a blessing in connection with this call. But what God asked Abram to do would not be easy. Abram was to leave his "country" (with all its familiar surroundings), to leave his "kindred" (uncles, aunts, and cousins), and even to leave his immediate family (his "father's house"). Abram was to go to a strange land and to dwell with a people he did not know. Yet "Abram went." Significantly, among the first things he did when he reached Canaan was to build "an altar to the LORD" (Genesis 12:7b).

WORDS FOR OUR TIME

Sometimes we hear people say something like, "Of course God could use Abram! Look at who he was," as though we were something less and therefore understandably and excusably less obedient. But nowhere do the Scriptures say God chose Abram because of any great qualities the man possessed. Abram came to be known as a person of unusual faith (Hebrews 11:8-12, 17-19), but that was because he responded to God's call. Abram was not described in this way when God called him. Indeed, Abram seems to have been an idol worshiper before the hand of God touched him (Joshua 24:2).

One of the proofs of just how human Abram was is revealed in the events Genesis 12:10-20 describes. In order to save his own skin, Abram concocted a lie and asked his wife, Sarai, to agree to it. Who would have thought it? The man who had come all the way from Haran because he was obeying God's command turns out to be a liar! True, Genesis 20:12 says that Sarai was Abram's half-sister; but even so, Abram's intent was to outwit and mislead Pharaoh. How easily we deceive by telling the truth but not the whole truth!

Although we would have liked for Abram to have been completely faithful to God, we do find hope for ourselves in Abram's failings. For if God can use a person like Abram, then God can use people today. If a man like Abram can become a person of faith, so can anyone. Abram stood condemned. He could not answer Pharaoh's charges. Abram apparently just stood there in embarrassed silence (Genesis 12:18-19).

However, you and I stand condemned too. Many times we stand mute in embarrassed silence before our Lord. But just as God renewed his call and his promise to Abram (Genesis 17:1-8 and other places), so also God renews his call to us. Abram always came back. What will we do, you and I?

WORDS FOR MY LIFE

It is all well and good for us to study about Abram and to marvel at the faith he displayed in answering God's call. But if we stop there, we have not yet understood what the Bible is trying to tell us.

The writers of the Bible had no real interest in lifting up heroes for us to admire. Rather, the Scriptures present us with pioneers to follow. What Abram did, we are called to do. We may or may not be asked to leave "country...and...kindred" in order to serve God, but we will surely be asked to leave security and comfort. Jesus said that if any would be followers of his, they must "deny themselves and take up their cross" (Matthew 16:24).

Deny ourselves. Take up our cross. Those words are not easy to obey. For Jesus' disciples, following them required that they begin a whole new way of life (Mark 1:17). For the rich man in Mark 10:17-22, beginning a new way of life was more than he was willing to do. For those who wanted to put their discipleship off until later, Jesus had strong words of rebuke (Luke 9:62). And for us, what will it be?

Let us note that in the very process of doing what God called him to do, Abram became a better person. He failed on occasion; but the more he obeyed, the less likely he was to disobey the next time. That first step must have been the hardest of all, for Abram had both comfort and security. Comfort and security are quite inviting. But I believe that few persons grow spiritually in such an atmosphere. It is only as we answer the call to the new and the untried that most of us make spiritual progress.

Let us also note that just as God promised Abram rewards for his obedience, so Christ offers us rewards. Abram left the land, the people, and the nation that he knew and loved. In return, he was given a new land and became the father of a new people. So also, says Jesus, "There is no one who has left house or brothers or sisters or mother or father or children or fields, for my sake and for the sake of the good news, who will not receive a hundredfold now in this age—houses...and fields...—and in the age to come eternal life" (Mark 10:29-30).

The story of Abram tells us that God calls whom he will, not necessarily the outstanding, but those who will hear and obey.

The story of Abram tells us that if we obey God, we will experience hardships, loneliness, and discouragement.

However, the story of Abram also tells us that God will bless those who obey. God will give them strength in times of need, intervene on their behalf during times of moral lapse, and use them for the most glorious task of all: to be a blessing to others.

3
MOSES ENCOUNTERS GOD

Exodus 3

God called to him out of the bush, "Moses, Moses!...Remove the sandals from your feet, for the place on which you are standing is holy ground....I have observed the misery of my people who are in Egypt; I have heard their cry....I know their sufferings, and I have come down to deliver them."   Exodus 3:4-8

WORDS FOR BIBLE TIMES

Do you remember the story of Moses' narrow escape from death as an infant? Put in a basket "lined with pitch and prayer," he floated among the bulrushes until Pharaoh's daughter discovered him. She gave him his name and took him to live with her at the palace, where he had all the comforts and advantages of royalty. Moses' own mother was brought in to be his nurse. It was no doubt from her that he learned of his true background and of the plight of his people.

One day, after Moses was grown, he saw an Egyptian beating one of the Hebrew slaves. Moses' anger so welled up within him that he killed the Egyptian and buried the body in the sand. But Moses' deed became known, and he had to flee to Midian for safety.

Moses' life in Midian was typical of that of the men around him. He married, had children, and worked as a shepherd. However, we can imagine that, in those long hours of solitude that every shepherd knows, Moses' thoughts often turned to the people he left behind. He undoubtedly relived many times the beating of that Hebrew slave and his own killing of the Egyptian taskmaster. The question of what could be done to free his people from such cruelty surely haunted him.

Then one day when he least expected it, Moses got his answer. He came to the mountain called Horeb, and there he saw a strange sight: a bush burning but not being consumed by the fire. As he turned aside to "look at this great sight" (Exodus 3:3), God called to him out of the bush, "I have observed the misery of my people" (Exodus 3:7).

How it must have thrilled Moses' heart to know that God had "come down to deliver" his people (Exodus 3:8)! But as Moses continued to listen, his mood changed to one of apprehension; for God said, "I will send you to Pharaoh to bring my people...out of Egypt" (Exodus 3:10). Moses had not counted on that.

Moses began to think of all the reasons he was not a good choice for

God's mission. For every objection he gave, however, God had an answer. "Who am I that I should go to Pharaoh?" asked Moses. Notice God's answer. Moses is not told, "You are the best person for the job," but rather, "I will be with you." Moses was still not convinced. "The people will want to know the name of the God who sent me," he said. "What shall I say to them?" "I AM WHO I AM," said God. "I AM has sent me to you." God promised, "They will listen to your voice." "So Moses took his wife and his sons . . . and went back to the land of Egypt" (Exodus 4:20).

WORDS FOR OUR TIME

A pastor I know likes to put the biblical stories in a modern setting and to tell them as if he had been directly involved in them. On one occasion he did this in his first sermon in a new appointment. He told the story of an oil refinery that had caught fire. Flames and smoke belched out so hot and so thick that fire fighters could not approach it. Then suddenly the fire stopped. To everyone's amazement the metal drums were cool, the surrounding grass was not scorched, and not a drop of oil had been consumed. He said that through that experience he heard God call him to be a pastor. This man reported later that the members of the congregation began to squirm noticeably as he told his story. They were obviously wondering, *What kind of a nut did the bishop send us as our preacher?* Nevertheless, he said that when they discovered he was really talking about Moses and the burning bush, suddenly everything was all right. Apparently the people felt it was OK for Moses to have an experience like that, but they did not want their pastor to.

The way those people felt raises some interesting questions. Did Moses really see a bush that was being burned but not consumed? If so, did the people of his day think he was "a nut"? Would Moses' call have been just as valid had he not seen the burning bush? In the Scriptures, fire often serves as a sign of God's presence. Can one ever describe a call from God without drawing on the symbolic? What constitutes a call from God anyway?

To try to explain the episode of the burning bush in psychological terms, as if the brooding of a sensitive soul had produced the whole experience, would be quite wrong. Moses was indeed sensitive to the hurts of his people, and his brooding unquestionably had prepared him for this theophany. However, theophany it was—a real and genuine manifestation of God to Moses. God made a divine invasion into Moses' life, uninvited and unexpected. And God came in order to call Moses into action.

So, to repeat, did people think of Moses as "a nut"? Some probably did. At first Moses himself thought the divine plan was unworkable. A call from God is always scary because it is a call to action and to the unknown. But those whom God calls he also equips for the task. "I will be with you," God told Moses; and Moses believed him. You and I are called to do the same.

WORDS FOR MY LIFE

How can we be sure what God is calling us to do? That question is not easy to answer. Certain things seem clear, however. First, when God calls, it is never for the purpose of our being able to bask in the glory of it all. If that is how we react to our call, we may be sure that we have either misunderstood or disobeyed the divine will. God calls because there is a job that needs to be done. Second, if we feel adequate for the job, we probably have substituted our own desires for God's will. God does not call us for the small, the easy, the trivial. God's call is to the seemingly impossible. But third, there is also the divine promise, "I will be with you." God's presence is what enables us to carry out the task. It is still scary, and it is still hard; but with God's help we can succeed. Fourth, although praise and adulation may be connected with our answering the call, we will certainly face opposition, hardships, and times of discouragement along the way. At times we may feel like giving up. But again comes the promise, "I will be with you"; and again the impossible becomes possible.

Many times we are reluctant to answer God's call, so we ask for a sign to make sure we have heard correctly. Sometimes God obliges us with such a sign; at other times no sign comes. God offered Moses a sign, but look at what it was! God said, "This shall be the sign for you...when you have brought the people out of Egypt, you shall worship God on this mountain" (Exodus 3:12). *"When you have brought"*—the sign, in other words, would not be given until the task had been completed. God was saying to Moses, "You must venture out on faith, and then I will give you a sign."

Moses went. And the surest sign that God was with him is the fact that he was able to complete the job God had given him to do. And so it will be with us.

4
THE TEN COMMANDMENTS

Exodus 20:1-17

God spoke all these words:

I am the LORD *your God, who brought you out of the land of Egypt, out of the house of slavery; you shall have no other gods before me.*

You shall not make for yourself an idol, whether in the form of anything that is in heaven above, or that is on the earth beneath, or that is in the water under the earth....

You shall not make wrongful use of the name of the LORD *your God, for the* LORD *will not acquit anyone who misuses his name.*

Remember the sabbath day, and keep it holy....

Honor your father and your mother, so that your days may be long in the land that the LORD *your God is giving you.*

You shall not murder.

You shall not commit adultery.

You shall not steal.

You shall not bear false witness against your neighbor.

You shall not covet your neighbor's house; you shall not covet your neighbor's wife, or male or female slave, or ox, or donkey, or anything that belongs to your neighbor.   Exodus 20:1-17

WORDS FOR BIBLE TIMES

Moses had successfully led the people out of Egypt. The confrontations with Pharaoh, the plagues, the parting of the sea—all that was behind them now. At first there had been an exhilaration about it all; but as the days wore on, that initial excitement began to fade. It was no picnic out there in the hot sun. The Hebrews had to go for long periods of time without water, and the food had not been all that regular either. The people "complained against Moses and Aaron," questioning both their motives and their leadership (Exodus 16:2-3).

Finally, "on the third new moon" after the children of Israel had left Egypt, they came into the wilderness of Sinai (Exodus 19:1). Moses had taken the people there because God had said that his sign to Moses would be that "when you have brought the people out of Egypt, you shall worship God on this mountain" (Exodus 3:12). After three more days had passed, a thick cloud came upon the mountain, accompanied by thunder and lightning; and God descended upon Mount Sinai in fire and smoke. The whole mountain quaked, and the people trembled with fear. It was in that awesome setting that God gave the people the Ten Commandments.

These commandments, particularly numbers five through nine, are so fundamental to an ordered society that they have become accepted almost everywhere in the world. But originally they were intended for a particular people. The Hebrews whom Moses had led out of Egypt had never known anything but slavery. How were they to live together in harmony? What would be their laws, their rules of conduct for everyday living? If these people were ever to become anything more than a collection of individual persons, and particularly if they were to become the people of God, such rules had to be established. God answered that need by giving them the Ten Commandments.

WORDS FOR OUR TIME

While recognizing the soundness of the Ten Commandments, some people have questioned their relevance for our day. These people point out that in our society almost everybody believes in only one God. We are not tempted to put other gods before the Lord or to make graven images for ourselves. Nor does the prohibition about working on the sabbath have much meaning for us. Having to work seven days a week is not our problem; rather, for most of us it is deciding what to do with our leisure time. Furthermore, there are some of the Ten Commandments that almost no one has any intention of keeping.

For instance, stealing and lying, it is said, are so prevalent in government, in industry, in advertising, and among individual persons that to root out these practices would be to alter our whole way of dealing with one another. The prevalence of child abuse makes us wonder if parents deserve our honor. Our society is so riddled with illicit sex in movies and in real life that the seventh commandment seems like a quaint, old-fashioned idea. So, of what value are the Ten Commandments as guidelines for life today?

This is a searching question, and we must face it honestly. Somehow it hardly seems sufficient to say simply that God's laws do not become antiquated. Yet in a very real sense this is the only answer we can give. What was good and right for the ancient Israelites as they stood at the foot of Mount Sinai is still right for us today. As one congregation heard from its pulpit, the commandments forbid "this thing, that thing, and the other thing" that we are so prone to do. It is a strange kind of logic that says that since our society is so riddled with a particular sin, we should do away with the commandment that forbids it. God's laws may take new shape and require new interpretations as the years go by, but they remain ever contemporary and ever authoritative. We forget that fact, or ignore it, at our peril.

WORDS FOR MY LIFE

Many scholars say that the first four commandments deal with religion, while the last six deal with ethics. That statement is both true and false. It is true that the first four commandments deal with how we are to relate to God, and the last six deal with how we are to relate to one another. But it is quite wrong to speak of these areas as though they were two separate categories. In the biblical understanding of things, ethics grow out of religion. It is precisely because we are children of God that God calls us to act toward others in the ways revealed in the Ten Commandments. That is why the Ten Commandments begin with an announcement of who is making these demands (Exodus 20:2). The same God who had taken the initiative in delivering the children of Israel from bondage in Egypt is now calling on the people to acknowledge his right to their sole allegiance. And a part of that allegiance is showing love and respect for God's human children.

The people of Israel recognized that God's rescue of them was an act of pure grace. They had no claim on God whatsoever. In fact, they had no reason even to suspect that God would come to their rescue. However, God came because of his great love and because of his promise made to their ancestor Abraham that he would give them a land of their own (Genesis 12:7, see Lesson 2). These are the only reasons the Bible ever gives for God's choice of the Israelites as a people "holy to the LORD" (Deuteronomy 7:6-8). These are the only reasons that can be given, for God's help was completely unmerited and unexpected. And in response to that love Israel bound itself to God in a covenant relationship and promised to keep God's laws. That is why the commandments dealing with our relation to God come first, and that is why it is totally inappropriate to try to separate the commandments into two categories, the one having to do with religion and the other with ethics.

If the ancient Hebrews had reason to be grateful for God's unmerited love toward them, how much more do you and I have reason to be grateful—we for whom Jesus Christ died on the cross. God saw our affliction too. God heard our cries of anguish, and God came down to deliver us, not out of the hand of the Egyptians, but out of the bondage of sin. And this coming down of God was just as unexpected and just as unmerited as was his coming to deliver the children of Israel. So we too bow before our God in humble gratitude. And we too pledge in our covenant with God that we shall not kill or steal, commit adultery, or in any other way harm those for whom Jesus Christ died.

5

THE GREAT COMMANDMENT

Deuteronomy 6:4-9

Hear, O Israel: The LORD is our God, the LORD alone. You shall love the LORD your God with all your heart, and with all your soul, and with all your might.

Deuteronomy 6:4-5

WORDS FOR BIBLE TIMES

Moses stands with the people of Israel gathered before him, and says, "Now this is the commandment—the statutes and the ordinances—that the LORD your God charged me to teach you" (Deuteronomy 6:1). Then he gives what Jesus called "the greatest commandment" (Matthew 22:36-38). This commandment is found in Deuteronomy 6:4-5. The steps that the people are to take to guarantee that Israel will never forget this commandment are given in verses 6-9.

Two things stand out in verses 6-9. First, the words of verses 4-5 are to become part and parcel of the everyday life of the Israelites. Wherever they are, whatever they are doing, the people are to keep these words constantly before them. They are to think of them when they first arise in the morning and when they go to bed at night. They are to remember these words when they are sitting at home and when they are walking by the way. They are to have physical reminders of these words by binding them on their hands and by wearing them on their foreheads. They are to write these words on the doorposts of their houses and on their gates. But most of all, they are to write them upon their hearts (verse 6). In that way this great commandment will become the guidepost of their lives.

Second, the Israelites are to teach these words to their children diligently. That is, parents are to impress the meaning and significance of this commandment on their children so the children will write these words on their hearts and think of them night and day. This emphasis is to continue to be made in each succeeding generation, for nothing is more crucial for a child to remember than the words of this commandment. Parents have no task that is more important than helping a child come to love God.

WORDS FOR OUR TIME

The idea of loving God, while not completely absent in other religions in Moses' day, was not a common understanding of the proper way to relate to the divine. People were to fear the gods, to seek to placate them, to obey them, and to worship them; but people were not to love them. However, time and time again in the Old Testament, Israel is called to love God. More often than not, the command to love God is followed by a command to keep God's laws.

That approach does not sound strange to us today. We are accustomed to the idea. Jesus said, "If you love me, you will keep my command-ments" (John 14:15). But the Old Testament writer did not have two thousand years of Christianity behind him. He was plowing new ground. Nevertheless, he was convinced that the proper reason for obey-ing God is because we love God, not because we are afraid of him or because we are seeking to gain some favor. This understanding in no way negates or diminishes the fact that we stand in awe of God and are to hold him in reverence. Not to stand in awe of God is to forget that he is God. However, God's nature is such that our primary response to him includes love and gratitude as well as awe. This love, this gratitude, and this awe lead us to obey God and to worship God.

Love is commitment. On a human level, when a man and a woman love each other deeply, their feelings may lead to a commitment that each makes to the other, a lifelong commitment. It is expressed on the human side through obedience. To "hear, O Israel" is not merely to com-prehend intellectually; it is to respond in obedience. For this reason, the later rabbis insisted that Deuteronomy 6:4-9, as well as Deuteronomy 11:13-21 and Numbers 15:37-41, be recited by Jewish males twice daily, once in the morning and once in the evening. On the sabbath, these words were used to open the synagogue service. Orthodox Jews, as well as some in the Conservative and Reform tradition, still follow these practices.

Many of us today do not practice any rituals in our homes or follow any patterns of behavior that would help us fasten our minds on God. Unfortunately, morning and evening devotions are largely a matter of the past, as are Bible reading, grace at meals, and regular times for instruc-tion in our homes on matters of faith. It is true that such practices can become ritual and nothing more. But one has to ask whether we have improved or impoverished the quality of our lives by giving them up.

WORDS FOR MY LIFE

Deuteronomy 6:5 calls us to love the Lord our God with all our heart and with all our soul and with all our might. The expression "with all your heart and with all your soul" appears several times in the Old

Testament. In Deuteronomy 4:29, for example, the value of searching for God "with all your heart and soul" is lifted up. Deuteronomy 10:12 speaks of serving God "with all your heart and with all your soul."

The Hebrews considered the heart to be the seat of will, of decision making, of determination. To love God with all the heart, then, was to determine that all your decisions would be made on the basis of faithfulness to God. To add "with all your might" to this expression is to say that you strongly determine—with all your might—that this will be so. People frequently point out that Jesus added the phrase "with all your mind" to this commandment (Mark 12:30). This addition was not an expansion of the commandment, however, but a clarification of it. In Hebrew thought the functions of the heart included determination and decision making. The addition of "with all your mind" is helpful in our time and language.

Verse 6 says these words shall be in our hearts. If the words are in our hearts, they are in our inner being. They well up from within us. They are a part of who we are. We live them because we want to, not because we are forced to do so (compare Jeremiah 31:31-34).

How do we get these words inscribed on our hearts? Verses 7-9 tell us. These verses tell us three quite important things. First, we are to make these words our constant companions. We need to have them in mind as we ride in automobiles or in jet planes, "at home . . . or away." Likewise, we need to think about eyeglasses and contact lenses, not frontlets, as reminders to love God always. If we are to receive the blessing promised in verse 3, we must find ways to keep these words in spirit. Verses 4-5 are to serve as our inspiration and motivation throughout the day. Second, we are to share these words with other people. We are to talk of God's love continually, to teach these words to our children, and to write these words in places where others are sure to see. Our faith and our love for God must be shared if they are genuine. Third, the binding of these words "as a sign on your hand" reminds us that the words are not to be just in our speech but in our deeds as well. God's love in our lives inspires our daily living, causes us to share the good news with our friends, and manifests itself in our deeds.

6
WE WILL SERVE THE LORD

Joshua 24:1-18

Now if you are unwilling to serve the LORD, choose this day whom you will serve, whether the gods your ancestors served in the region beyond the River or the gods of the Amorites in whose land you are living; but as for me and my household, we will serve the LORD.   Joshua 24:15

WORDS FOR BIBLE TIMES

Joshua has asked "all the tribes of Israel" to gather at Shechem (Joshua 24:1). Obviously something quite important is about to happen. The elders, the heads of the families, the judges, and the officers of Israel present themselves. Then Joshua speaks. But his very first words are "Thus says the LORD" (verse 2). The words he is about to say are not the words of a mere mortal. God is actually addressing the assembly.

God is going to call attention to all that he has done for the people, beginning with the time of the patriarchs (verses 2-4). God reminds the people that their ancestors had worshiped "other gods" before he laid his hand on Abraham and led him through the land of Canaan. Through a miraculous birth, God gave Abraham and Sarah a son, Isaac. Through Isaac, God made Abraham's offspring "many." To Isaac, God gave Jacob and Esau. God gave Esau and his descendants "the hill country of Seir." But Jacob and his family "went down to Egypt." In verses 5-7, God recalls what he did to rescue the descendants of Jacob from Egypt. Then, in verse 8, God says, "I brought you to the land of the Amorites." Verses 8-13 recount what God has done for the people since they have been in the Promised Land. Verse 13 emphasizes the desirability of the land and the complete dependence of the Israelites on God for all the good things they now enjoy.

Then comes the crux of the matter: "Now therefore revere the LORD, and serve him in sincerity and in faithfulness" (verse 14). Notice the word *therefore*. It is because of what God has done for the people that they are now being asked to give their allegiance to the Almighty. God is not asking them to do anything other than what could reasonably be expected. However, their choice is not between serving God or serving no god at all; it is between serving God or serving other gods. So Joshua says, "Put away the gods that your ancestors served beyond the River and in Egypt, and serve the LORD" (verse 14b).

That is why this assembly was called. The time had come for a renewing of the covenant between the people of Israel and God. Most of the persons who initially made the covenant were now dead. Sons and daughters and even grandchildren now had to assume the responsibilities of the covenant for themselves. Furthermore, even those who had been faithful to God needed a chance to renew their commitment. This covenant renewal service provided for that too.

WORDS FOR OUR TIME

The challenge had been put before the people, and they had to make a decision. Joshua himself led the way. "If you are unwilling to serve the LORD," he said, "choose this day whom you will serve, whether the gods your ancestors served in the region beyond the River or the gods of the Amorites in whose land you are living; but as for me and my household, we will serve the LORD" (verse 15).

The people responded to the challenge. They recognized that it was the Lord, not the gods of their fathers or the Amorite gods, who had delivered them and protected them all these years. "Far be it from us that we should forsake the LORD to serve other gods," they said (verse 16). "We also will serve the LORD" (verse 18).

Most people might think that Joshua would have been pleased at the Israelites' decision. But listen to his words: "You cannot serve the LORD, for he is a holy God. He is a jealous God; he will not forgive your transgressions or your sins" (verse 19). Joshua knew how easy it is to get caught up in the emotions of the moment. He knew that a commitment based on emotions and nothing more is not likely to survive the tests that come to all of us. He had to make sure the people really meant what they were saying. If you begin to follow God, he warned, and then turn away from him, God will "consume you" even though he has "done you good" in the past. We are reminded of Jesus' words: "No one who puts a hand to the plow and looks back is fit for the kingdom of God" (Luke 9:62). Once our hand is on the plow, we must till a straight row.

We need to be reminded of that fact today. Most of us find it easy to make promises to God when our emotions are at a high pitch. But such promises will surely be strewn along the walkways of life unless they come from a sincere, committed, and determined heart. Joshua had to make sure the people understood the seriousness of their promise to God.

The people assured Joshua that they were fully aware of what their promise meant and that they were fully determined to carry it through.

They took an oath against themselves that they would be true to their pledge. "So Joshua made a covenant with the people that day" (verse 25).

WORDS FOR MY LIFE

When Joshua said to the people, "Choose this day whom you will serve," he packed three quite important ideas into seven brief words. First, he said, "Choose." Life demands decisions. However, many of us would rather drift through life, letting others make our decisions for us. We drift into a vocation, drift into relationships, drift into—or out of— the church. Joshua pointed out the importance of taking the responsibility for making our own decisions.

Second, he said, "Choose this day." There are times when it is appropriate to delay a decision. Most people have had the experience of regretting a decision they made in haste. Nevertheless, there also comes a time when the decision must be made or it is too late. Joshua was convinced that his people were at that point. They had promised long ago to follow God and only God, yet many of them were still worshiping idols (verse 23). The time had come for them to make a firm commitment, one way or the other. "How long will you go limping with two different opinions?" Elijah asked the people of his day. "If the LORD is God, follow him; but if Baal, then follow him" (1 Kings 18:21). And that is exactly what Joshua was saying.

Third, Joshua said, "Choose this day whom you will serve." No decision we make is more important than that one. Most people today are not tempted to worship idols, yet we are tempted to make "gods" out of the things of this world. Jesus said, "You cannot serve God and wealth" (Matthew 6:24); yet how hard we try to do just that! We want to make a million dollars *and* to be loyal to Christ. We want to serve the church *and* to serve ourselves. But Joshua reminds us, even as Jesus Christ himself did, that we must "choose this day whom [we] will serve."

7
WHERE YOU GO, I WILL GO

Ruth 1:1-18; 4:13-17

Do not press me to leave you
or to turn back from following you!
Where you go, I will go;
where you lodge, I will lodge;
your people shall be my people,
and your God my God.   Ruth 1:16

WORDS FOR BIBLE TIMES

It was not easy to leave family and friends and go to a new land. But in times of drought there is not always a choice. So Elimelech and Naomi and their two sons gathered what belongings they could carry and headed for Moab. The trip from Bethlehem was only about sixty miles, but sixty miles can seem like six hundred when the earth is parched and it is far into the night before the air cools.

The family arrived safely in Moab and settled there. However, adversity was soon to strike again: Elimelech died. In due time Naomi's two sons, Mahlon and Chilion, took Moabite wives named Orpah and Ruth. But in about ten years, Mahlon and Chilion died, leaving Orpah and Ruth to live with Naomi.

The ancient world did not offer much protection for widows. They were at the mercy of those around them. So when Naomi heard that the drought was over in Judah, she decided to return to her homeland. She had friends and family there.

Naomi set out for Bethlehem. Orpah and Ruth accompanied her. But somewhere along the way Naomi set her daughters-in-law free from their obligation to go with her. She knew what it was like to be a widow in a strange land, and she did not want Orpah and Ruth to have to endure that. Naomi said, in effect, "Go back home, and may you find a place in the home of your husbands."

However, both women refused. "We will return with you to your people," they said (Ruth 1:10).

Naomi insisted that they turn back. She told them to return to their own people, find new husbands, and live happily there.

Orpah could see the wisdom in Naomi's words. With tears in her eyes, she kissed her beloved mother-in-law and returned to her homeland.

—— 25 ——

But Ruth would not. "Go," Naomi said to her. "See, your sister-in-law has gone back. Return with her."

Then Ruth spoke these beautiful and immortal words:

> "Do not press me to leave you
>   or to turn back from following you!
> Where you go, I will go;
>   where you lodge, I will lodge;
> your people shall be my people,
>   and your God my God.
> Where you die, I will die—
>   there will I be buried." (Ruth 1:16-17)

When Naomi saw Ruth's love and devotion and determination, she said no more.

WORDS FOR OUR TIME

Being a widow is not easy today. But in the ancient world it was even more difficult. Widows were easy targets for the unscrupulous male and often were exploited, both for sexual favors and for financial gain. Widows had no rights and were entirely dependent on their family for support. Naomi, a sojourner in Moab, had no family there. Her only recourse was to return to Judah. Likewise, Ruth's lot in Judah would be no better than Naomi's in Moab. Ruth would be a widow, a sojourner, and would have no rights. Her only protection would be from Naomi's family.

The Book of Ruth has a happy ending because of a custom in ancient Israel. According to this custom, the next of kin had the right to buy the land and the property of a deceased relative. If the next of kin chose not to buy the property, the right to buy fell to the second closest kin, and on down the line. Included in the "property" was the widow of the deceased.

Naomi took it upon herself to get Boaz (a kinsman of her deceased husband), who was both wealthy and unmarried, interested enough in Ruth to buy Elimelech's property, including the right to marry Ruth. Into that marriage was born a baby who was given the name *Obed*. The entire family rejoiced.

However, the point of the story has not yet been made. The Book of Ruth is not just a pleasant story about a woman of Judah who had to sojourn in Moab, who had several brushes with misfortune, who returned to Judah with her daughter-in-law, and who was then able to see her daughter-in-law marry into wealth and happiness. This story would be pleasant enough if that were all it was. But the real point of the story comes in the last sentence of Ruth 4:17: "They named him Obed; he became the father of Jesse, the father of David." The son of an alien woman was to become the grandfather of the greatest king Israel ever had and a forebear of Jesus Christ.

We have not outgrown all prejudice against those who are different. Are there not those whose race, nationality, religious affiliation, or other differences make them unwelcome in certain positions? Some groups of persons have never had—and never will have in our lifetime—a major candidate for president or vice-president of the U.S. Some types of "aliens" would be unwelcome as a pastor, as a personal physician, or as an in-law. We still need pioneers to break the stereotypes and to influence our time as Ruth influenced Israel.

WORDS FOR MY LIFE

The Book of Ruth begins with a famine; it ends with a blessing (Ruth 4:14-15). The book begins with the deaths of Elimelech and Mahlon and Chilion; it ends with the births of Obed and Jesse and David. Things get so bad for Naomi that she says, "Call me Mara," which means bitter, rather than Naomi, which means pleasant (Ruth 1:20). But in the end she rejoices at the birth of Obed, and her friends rejoice with her.

We do not like adversity, you and I. The minor inconveniences in our lives irritate us, and we feel resentful when major difficulties come to us. We like for things to go our way, and we like our sailing to be smooth. But like Naomi and Ruth, we sometimes discover that the best things in life come after a period of hardship. Indeed, the best things in life sometimes come as a result of the time of pain. Without the famine, Naomi and Elimelech would never have gone to Moab. Except for the trip to Moab, Mahlon and Chilion would never have married Moabite wives (Jews were strongly prejudiced against Moabites). Except for the deaths of the three husbands, Naomi would not have returned to Judah. Had Naomi not returned to Judah, Ruth would not have married Boaz. Without the marriage to Boaz, Obed would not have been born. And without the birth of Obed, David would not have been born. Without the birth of David, the history of Jews and Christians alike would have been changed drastically.

Perhaps you and I cannot trace the good in our lives back through such a series of events, but can we not all think of certain blessings that have come to us after some misfortune came our way? God has a way of using the worst to bring about the best. The most creative period in the history of ancient Israel was during the worst calamity the people ever suffered—the Babylonian exile. The times when you and I reach our deepest insights and come to trust God the most may be those times when outward circumstances are the least favorable. God uses such experiences to mold our character and to prepare us for the future. Both Naomi and Ruth received far more than they lost when affairs seemed to turn against them. The same is often true for us.

8
A SOUND OF SHEER SILENCE

1 Kings 19:1-18

Now there was a great wind, so strong that it was splitting mountains and breaking rocks in pieces before the LORD, but the LORD was not in the wind; and after the wind an earthquake, but the LORD was not in the earthquake; and after the earthquake a fire, but the LORD was not in the fire; and after the fire a sound of sheer silence.

1 Kings 19:11-12

WORDS FOR BIBLE TIMES

Elijah, whose prophetic efforts often had been a lonely voice battling against both the crown and popular opinion, had finally won the day. In a dramatic confrontation on top of Mount Carmel, Elijah had demonstrated beyond a doubt that it was the God of Israel who controlled the forces of nature and not the pagan god Baal. Fire had come down out of heaven and had consumed the offering on the altar. The people had confessed that the Lord is God. The false prophets were gone. The rains, which had not fallen for three years, poured out on the land (1 Kings 18:17-45).

Every reformer dreams of this kind of day. However, little did Elijah know that he was about to face the severest test of his life.

When word reached the queen, Jezebel, of what had happened, she sent a message to Elijah, saying, in effect, "As sure as you are Elijah and I am Jezebel, you will be dead by this time tomorrow!" (1 Kings 19:2). Terror struck Elijah's heart, and he began to run. He did not stop until he came to Beer-sheba at the southern tip of Judah, a journey of more than one hundred miles. Leaving his servant there, Elijah traveled a day's journey into the desert alone. Exhausted by his trip and despondent over the turn of events in his life, Elijah sat under a broom tree and prayed that he might die. "I am no better than my ancestors," he said (verse 4), no more successful than they in ridding the land of Baalism. Elijah then lay down, and sleep overcame him. The next thing he knew, an angel awakened him and told him to eat. There in front of Elijah were a cake and a jar of water. He satisfied his desire for food and drink and then traveled "forty days and forty nights" on the strength of it until he reached Mount Horeb (verse 8). There he came to a cave and went inside.

WORDS FOR OUR TIME

What happened to Elijah next was important, not only for his life, but for our lives as well. The encounter with God began with a question: "What are you doing here, Elijah?" (verse 9). How good it would be to know the tone of God's voice when God spoke those words. Was it a tone of displeasure and censure? Or was that question God's way of getting Elijah to think through his own motives and his understanding of God? Elijah answered, "I have been very zealous for the LORD" (verse 10). Elijah's words plainly implied, "but nobody else has." As for the others, they have "forsaken your covenant, thrown down your altars, and killed your prophets with the sword. I alone am left, and they are seeking my life, to take it away" (verse 10).

God would have some important words for Elijah to hear. But first there was a lesson Elijah needed to learn. So God caused "a great wind" to come, a wind so powerful it tore pieces of rock from the mountain (verse 11). Elijah undoubtedly expected to find God in that wind, for God had come in such a way during Elijah's victory over the prophets of Baal on Mount Carmel. But lo, God was not in the wind. Then there came a great earthquake. Surely God would be in the earthquake, for this very mountain had quaked when God had come to Moses (Exodus 19:18). But God was not in the earthquake either. Then a great fire came. God had descended to Moses in a fire, but it was not to be this time. God was not in the fire. Discouraged and broken, Elijah no doubt wondered if God were going to come to him at all. But then it happened! Elijah heard a "sound of sheer silence" (verse 12). It was nothing more than stillness; but there was no mistake about it—God was in that silence. God had come to Elijah, not in the sensational and the spectacular, but in a "sound of sheer silence."

That was a lesson Elijah needed to learn, for he was a thunderous person himself; and he conceived of God as being a thunderous God. In the past God had indeed spoken to his people in the spectacular, and God would do so again. But Elijah needed to learn that was not the only way, perhaps not even the most frequent way, God speaks to God's people. God also comes in the "sound of sheer silence."

WORDS FOR MY LIFE

Another lesson God had for Elijah came in the words God spoke to him. First, God said to Elijah, "Go" (verse 15). Whenever God calls a person, it is because God has a job for that person to do. Obedience always involves "going" somewhere, either to a new place or to a different way to approach a familiar situation. Elijah had been ready to quit; he even prayed that he might die. But God was not through with Elijah yet. There were other things for him to do. So God's word to Elijah was "Go."

Second, Elijah had been wrong when he said, "I alone am left" among the worshipers of the true God. We should not be surprised that Elijah felt that way. We often feel very much alone in this world. We are especially prone to such moods when we are discouraged and more especially when we are physically exhausted as well. But God had some news for Elijah—he was not alone. Not only was God still with him, there were also "seven thousand" others who had never "bowed to Baal" or kissed one of his images (verse 18). The road is never as lonely as it looks. And that is God's message to us as well as to Elijah. God is still with us and so are "seven thousand" others.

Another part of the lesson was when God told Elijah, "When you arrive [in Damascus], you shall anoint Hazael...Jehu...and...Elisha" (verses 15-16). The point here is that God works through human beings to get his work done in the world. Elijah had called on God to work through nature, to send fire down from heaven and rains to water the earth. Elijah was right in saying that the Lord, rather than Baal, was the God of nature. "God created the heavens and the earth" (Genesis 1:1), and "the heavens are telling the glory of God" (Psalm 19:1). But after we have said that, there is still more to say; for God is not only, or even primarily, a God of nature. He is a God of relationships. God made men and women in his image. God made a covenant with his people. It is through human beings that God most often gives guidance and blessings to people.

That is not to say that God never works through marvelous displays of power. But far more often it seems that God chooses the method of the "sound of sheer silence," telling the faithful what needs to be done and relying on them to "go" do it. Elijah needed to learn that. And God will not object if you and I eavesdrop on Elijah's experience so we can learn that lesson too.

9
FOR JUST SUCH A TIME AS THIS

Esther 4

Who knows? Perhaps you have come to royal dignity for just such a time as this.
Esther 4:14

WORDS FOR BIBLE TIMES

Haman was quite proud of himself. After all, he had been promoted to second-in-command of the entire Persian Empire. People bowed to him as he went by—everyone, that is, except a certain Jew named Mordecai. Haman was furious at Mordecai and determined that he should pay dearly for such insolence. Not being satisfied with punishing Mordecai only, Haman sought and received approval from the king to have all the Jews in the kingdom annihilated.

The edict went out that all the Jews were to be killed on the thirteenth day of the month of Adar. What the king did not know was that his wife, Queen Esther, was a Jew. Indeed, she was the niece of Mordecai. The edict that Haman had sent out brought on Mordecai's mourning, with which Esther 4 begins.

Esther knew nothing of Haman's order until her attendants told her that Mordecai had donned sackcloth and ashes and was wailing with a loud voice in the midst of the city. She immediately sent word to him to come to see her. However, Mordecai could not enter the king's gate while dressed in sackcloth; and he refused the change of clothing that Esther sent to him. Esther, therefore, had to talk to Mordecai through a messenger; and it was from this messenger that Esther learned of Haman's order.

Mordecai implored Esther to ask the king to rescind Haman's order, but Esther feared for her life. She reminded Mordecai that no one could approach the king unless summoned by him. Anyone who violated this law risked death. And the king had not summoned Esther for a month. Esther was afraid that she had fallen out of favor with the king and that he would not welcome any attempt that she might make to see him.

Mordecai's reply to Esther contained both a bit of wisdom and a stirring challenge. The wisdom was this: Do not think you will escape death if all the Jews are annihilated; for you too are a Jew, and that fact will certainly be discovered. The challenge was this: Here is your chance to save all the Jews in the kingdom. "Who knows? Perhaps you have come to royal dignity for just such a time as this" (Esther 4:14).

Mordecai's words persuaded Esther. She was convinced that it was her duty to approach the king. She knew her life would be in danger, but she also knew she must do it. "If I perish," she said, "I perish" (Esther 4:16).

WORDS FOR OUR TIME

Many people think the Book of Esther has no religious value. They say that the book is a purely secular story with secular values and no mention of religion. The book can certainly be read in that way. Nowhere in the entire book is God mentioned. Nowhere do we find any reference to prayer or to worship or to any of the great religious festivals of Judaism. The motives of the people seem to be nonreligious, self-serving, and exclusivistic. But the fact that God is not mentioned in the book does not mean that God is not active in the events described. The careful reader can discern God's hand in much of the story. No one knows why the author chose not to mention God. Many scholarly guesses have been made, but none of them is entirely satisfactory. Be that as it may, there are several places in the book where God and religious practices seem to be spoken of indirectly; and one of those places is in Chapter 4 in the words of Modecai.

"Who knows?" asked Mordecai. "Perhaps you have come to royal dignity for just such a time as this." What better expression of God's providential care could we ask for than that? Chapter 2 gives an account of Esther's being chosen as queen. That chapter gives not the slightest hint that God had anything to do with the king's choice of Esther. She was chosen on the basis of her beauty. Mordecai had schemed to get her in the contest, perhaps; and he advised her not to make known the fact that she was a Jew. But after that she was on her own. She found favor in the eyes of Hegai, who attended the women; and she followed the tips he gave her. Esther also found favor in the eyes of the king. The crown was placed on her head, and she became queen of the empire.

However, behind it all, Mordecai's words suggest that God was guiding the events and bringing about the king's selection of Esther. At a point when it became quite important to have someone in a position of authority to protect the Jews from Haman's decree, Esther was there.

WORDS FOR MY LIFE

You and I often experience the same thing that happened to Esther. Something happens to us, and it seems like a normal event in the course of our lives. But later the knowledge we gained through that experience proves to be exactly what we need for a task we have to face. We often remark, "I didn't realize it at the time, but now I can see that God was preparing me for the job I had to do" (or words to that effect).

Even after we have been prepared for our task, however, it is up to us to perform it. The Jews would not have been helped and the story of Esther would never have been written if Esther had not agreed to lay her life on the line. Some people have criticized Esther because her first thoughts after hearing Mordecai's challenge were of her own safety rather than the welfare of her people. But let us not be too quick to condemn her. After all, she was asked to risk her very life. Would we have been willing to do that? Most of us complain if we are asked to be inconvenienced a little for the sake of other people. What would our response be if we were asked to place our head in the gallows' noose on behalf of someone else?

Yet that is exactly what Christ calls us to do. "If any want to become my followers," said Jesus, "let them deny themselves and take up their cross and follow me" (Mark 8:34). We tend to try to "spiritualize" those words, to make them nothing more than a metaphor. When some unpleasant task comes our way, we often speak of it as being the cross we have to bear. But the cross is a symbol of death. When Jesus said we must take up our cross, he was saying that we must be willing to be nailed to it. Our commitment to him is to be so strong that we are prepared to die for him if called to do so.

The choices we have to face in life may never be that radical. You and I may never be asked to lay down our life for God. But our call is to be willing to do so if the situation demands it.

That was Esther's call too. And she met the challenge. She did not like the prospect of losing her life. She would have preferred an easier way. But that was her call, and she answered it. "I will go to the king," she said. "And if I perish, I perish" (Esther 4:16). Can we do less for our Lord?

10
THE LORD IS MY SHEPHERD

Psalm 23

The LORD is my shepherd, I shall not want.
He makes me lie down in green pastures;
he leads me beside still waters;
he restores my soul.
He leads me in right paths
for his name's sake.

Even though I walk through the darkest valley,
I fear no evil;
for you are with me;
your rod and your staff—
they comfort me.

You prepare a table before me
in the presence of my enemies;
you anoint my head with oil;
my cup overflows.
Surely goodness and mercy shall follow me
all the days of my life,
and I shall dwell in the house of the LORD
my whole life long.

Psalm 23

WORDS FOR BIBLE TIMES

Obviously, only a shepherd could have written the Twenty-third Psalm. Another word needs to be added, however. Only a *good* shepherd could have written it. The psalmist was a good shepherd, knowing exactly what the sheep needed and having a loving concern for them. But these truths came out only incidentally, for the psalmist did not write about himself but about God. It is true, as many have pointed out, that the words *I, me,* and *my* occur a total of eighteen times in this brief psalm. But the psalmist had to use these personal pronouns to express his thanks. God had taken care of him even as a shepherd takes care of his sheep.

The shepherd's job was to provide for the sheep's needs and to protect the sheep from harm. If the shepherd was a good shepherd, the sheep would not "want." That is, all their needs would be taken care of. The good shepherd caused his sheep to "lie down in green pastures" where the new, tender grasses were growing. He led the sheep to the "still waters" where they could drink in comfort and in safety. Refreshed and restored, they could once again make their way to another pasture or back to the fold.

The good shepherd made sure that he led his sheep in the right paths. Doing so was not always easy in ancient Israel. The night shadows gathered quickly in the ravines and in the mountain passes. Sheep could get lost there; wild animals often lurked there; and thieves lay in wait there for the unsuspecting traveler and for the shepherd returning home with his flock. So the shepherd had to know all the right paths and how to avoid the dangerous ones. As an added precaution, he carried both a "rod" and a "staff," the one for protection, the other for guiding wayward sheep. All these duties are mentioned or alluded to in four short verses. The person who wrote this psalm was intimately acquainted with the life of a shepherd, and every verse reveals his love for the sheep.

WORDS FOR OUR TIME

The last two verses of this psalm have caused a great deal of debate among scholars. The issue is whether the scene changes or whether the setting is still in green pastures beside still waters. If the scene changes, where are we—in a banquet hall or in the Temple? And if the scene does not change, who are we? Are we still sheep being cared for by the good shepherd, or are we travelers receiving hospitality from a desert host? Let us consider two of these possibilities, first changing the scene to a banquet hall and then changing the image to that of a weary traveler.

To the modern reader of this psalm, it seems obvious that a change of scenery occurs in verse 5. No longer is the psalmist in the meadow or climbing the mountain pass. He is now attending a banquet. It is not clear why the psalmist's "enemies" are near. But there they are. They watch in envy as the psalmist enjoys the best in food and drink, served by a host who makes sure that his guest's cup is filled to overflowing. In ancient Israel hosts customarily anointed their guests with soothing oils. This host, gracious beyond compare, does so. You may recall that Jesus' host on one occasion was not as considerate of his guest's needs (Luke 7:46).

It is not necessary, however, to make such a radical change of scenery; for the shepherd of biblical days not only tended the sheep under his care but also acted as host to weary desert travelers. Perhaps what we have here is a picture of the shepherd acting in both these capacities. In verses 1-4, he cares for the sheep; and in verses 5-6, he acts as host for the traveler. If so, the psalmist changes roles at verse 5, going from a sheep being fed by still waters to a traveler being feted until his cup overflows. And because the shepherd offers protection as well as a place to eat and rest, the traveler can eat in safety even though his enemies are near. The shepherd, as host, then spreads soothing oil on the stranger's head.

In our society, we are suspicious of strangers. Such hospitality is little known and rarely practiced. We feel that we do not have time to care for other people's needs. We say that it would be irresponsible to spend our time and resources on someone we do not even know. Our family needs our help. Or so we claim.

WORDS FOR MY LIFE

Coming out of a pastoral background and being quite familiar with the needs of the sheep and the duties of the shepherd, this psalmist boldly declares, "The LORD is my shepherd"! Certainly, therefore, "I shall not want." And though the psalmist probably was referring to "right paths" and the "darkest valley" in verses 3 and 4, it is entirely appropriate for Christians to extend the meaning to include "paths of righteousness" and "the valley of the shadow of death" (see the footnotes in the New Revised Standard Version of the Bible). For our Lord, who was himself the Good Shepherd (John 10:14), is our guide and our comfort in all of life. If we follow him, we will stay on the paths of righteousness; and he will see us through the valley of death.

This psalm does not say that we will never experience adversity. The psalmist did not expect paths without shadows. But he would "fear no evil," he said, "even though" there were dark paths, "for you are with me." Nor does our Lord guarantee us that our paths will always be lighted. But he does guarantee that he will be there with us to guide, to protect, and to sustain.

The Twenty-third Psalm has another implication, however, that we should not overlook. Sheep are entirely dependent on the shepherd for their safe return to the fold. Left to themselves, sheep wander off, get lost, and lay themselves open to all kinds of danger. We are no better, you and I. We wander off the "right paths" too. We get spiritually lost, and we expose ourselves to all kinds of danger. It is only because the shepherd leads that we can "fear no evil."

Notice too that the psalmist says it was the shepherd's "rod" and "staff" that brought him "comfort." The rod we can understand. That was the shepherd's weapon for fighting off the wild beasts. But the shepherd used his staff to discipline the sheep. The sheep could sometimes be stubborn in their insistence on going the wrong way. And though a good shepherd would try to be as gentle as possible in dealing with his sheep, there were times when he had to use the staff with force. It was that staff that the psalmist said brought him comfort. For he understood that "all we like sheep have gone astray" (Isaiah 53:6). He knew that without the shepherd's staff, he would never make it to the "green pastures."

And what about us? We often resent it when the staff of discipline is used on us. Do we have something to learn from this psalmist?

11
THE SUFFERING SERVANT

Isaiah 52:13–53:12

Surely he has borne our infirmities
and carried our diseases;
yet we accounted him stricken,
struck down by God, and afflicted.
But he was wounded for our transgressions,
crushed for our iniquities;
upon him was the punishment that made us whole,
and by his bruises we are healed.

Isaiah 53:4-5

WORDS FOR BIBLE TIMES

The nation of Judah came to an end in 586 B.C. The Babylonian army overran the land, destroyed the buildings, and took the people into exile. They never dreamed that such a thing could happen. As long ago as the time of Abraham, it was understood that they were God's chosen people, that through them "all the families of the earth" would be blessed (Genesis 12:3). But look at them. How could they be a blessing to anybody, this defeated and humiliated nation? The poem we are studying in this lesson was written at a time when this mood of despair hung over the Israelites.

This magnificent poem is the crown of Old Testament theology. In fact, it is New Testament theology found within the Old Testament. The prophet wanted his people to realize that God could still use them to accomplish the divine purpose. Much to their surprise, the prophet indicated that they were in a better position now to bless the nations than ever before. To help them understand, he told them the story of someone God called "my servant" (Isaiah 52:13).

The servant grew up as one who did not attract attention. Nothing about him caused people to feel close to him or to think highly of him. He was, in fact, despised and rejected by those around him. At some point in his life he was "struck down by God" as well (Isaiah 53:4). Indeed, he was afflicted to such an extent that his appearance was "marred...beyond human semblance" (Isaiah 52:14). In the minds of the people that could mean only one thing; for according to their way of thinking, only those whose sins were very great received such severe punishment.

— 39 —

But then there came a revelation from God, a revelation so stirring that those who had scoffed at the servant could not believe what they heard. The servant was suffering, not for his own sins, but for theirs. The servant was innocent, yet he voluntarily took on himself the punishment due those who had wronged him. Moreover, God's plan from the beginning had been that the world would be blessed through the servant's suffering. After the servant's period of suffering, he would be "exalted and lifted up" (Isaiah 52:13). The "will of the LORD" would prosper (Isaiah 53:10). The servant would "see light" "out of his anguish," and he would "find satisfaction" (Isaiah 53:11).

Such was the dream of this great prophet. He was calling on his people to be that servant. He was saying to them that it was not too late for Israel to fulfill its destiny. "The nations have scorned us, battered us, and brought us to shame," he was saying. "But by taking on ourselves the punishment due them, we can be God's agent through whom the world will be redeemed." What a challenge he put before his people.

WORDS FOR OUR TIME

You and I know that the people did not accept this challenge. Rather than enduring their suffering graciously, they became exclusivistic and intolerant of others. When allowed to return to their homeland, they did not open up their hearts to the people there but instead insisted that Jews separate and isolate themselves from all others. They spurned the offer of the Samaritan people to help them rebuild the Temple (Ezra 4:1-3). They required that any Jewish man who had married a non-Jew must "put away" both his wife and all the children she had borne him (Ezra 10:3-5). The people of Israel seemed to be taking a path directly opposite to the one to which they had been called. As the years rolled by it appeared less and less likely that this great prophet's dream would ever be fulfilled.

However, this "dream" was not just the result of a prophet's overactive imagination; it was God's plan to save the world. And God does not allow his purposes to be thwarted by the sinfulness of his people. Thus there came a day when a baby boy was born, and they "named him Jesus" (Matthew 1:25). It was this Jesus, when he became an adult, who took on himself the sins of the world. It was he who was despised and rejected by those he sought to save. It was he who went to the cross on our behalf. And it was he whom death could not hold.

The dream had come true at last. But God has a way of fulfilling prophetic hopes even beyond the prophet's wildest dreams. Jesus, the suffering servant, was also the Christ, the Incarnation of God. God himself suffered in order to redeem his people. "Thanks be to God," said Paul, "for his indescribable gift!" (2 Corinthians 9:15).

WORDS FOR MY LIFE

As we look at this moving passage of Scripture, we are amazed at the insight of this great prophet. Almost six centuries before Jesus was born, this prophet could envision and understand God's plans to a remarkable degree. What a spiritual giant he was! Yet how lonely and painful his life must have been. He saw what others failed to see. He agonized over what others took for granted. This great prophet was so far ahead of his time that the world had to wait almost six hundred years for his dream to become a reality.

Christians rejoice in the fact that Jesus Christ fulfilled the dream of this great prophet. To read in Paul's letters that God has "highly exalted" Christ and given him "the name that is above every name" (Philippians 2:9) is quite thrilling. The rewards promised to the servant are heaped on Christ, and we find great comfort in that. But we know the world is not perfect. The prophet's dream has not yet been fulfilled in its entirety. The world is waiting for yet more servants.

Jesus Christ calls us to be those servants. As his followers, we are to hear the pain, the humiliation, even the death sentence, if necessary, that rightfully belong to others. A part of what it means to be a follower of Jesus Christ is to take up our cross (Matthew 10:38). Jesus said, "If they persecuted me, they will persecute you" (John 15:20).

Considering such a challenge and such consequences, we can better understand why the people of ancient Israel failed. It is easy to want to see right prevail in the world, but it is quite another matter to be willing to suffer in order to make it happen. The people of Israel were not quite ready to travel such a high road. They chose the lesser way. You and I are also invited to share the servant role with Jesus. But doing so would mean bearing our cross as he bore his. Are we willing? Shall we do it? Which road shall *we* take?

12
A NEW COVENANT

Jeremiah 31:31-34

The days are surely coming, says the LORD, when I will make a new covenant with the house of Israel and the house of Judah....I will put my law within them, and I will write it on their hearts.   Jeremiah 31:31, 33

WORDS FOR BIBLE TIMES

Who would have thought it would have come to this: God's own people, destroyed? God had rescued them from Egypt, had made a covenant with them, had protected them throughout their wanderings in the wilderness, had given them a land to live in, and had stayed by their side all these years. What a thrilling history it was! But then the Babylonian army attacked. And now look—the nation was devastated, the Temple was in ruins, the people were in exile. Why, God? What went wrong?

Various people gave the usual unsatisfactory answers: God had been defeated by the god(s) of Babylonia, or God just did not care about his people anymore. But the more discerning of Judah's people knew that these answers were far awry. The truth was, God was punishing the people of Judah for their sins. The nation had made a covenant with God a long time ago. The Hebrews had agreed to give God first place in their lives, to worship God only, and to obey God's laws. But the people had not lived up to that covenant. Their history could be written as a series of broken promises to God. Amos had warned the Hebrews more than a century earlier that God destroys evil nations. The fall of the Northern Kingdom in 722/21 B.C. had proved that Amos was right. Why then should the people of the Southern Kingdom, Judah, be surprised about what had happened to them? God simply could not allow such sin to go unchecked.

However, to a sensitive soul like Jeremiah, even this answer was incomplete. Nobody knew better than he that Judah had broken the covenant. The people of Judah, he said, were an "evil people," a people who "refuse to hear" God's word to them and who "stubbornly follow their own will" (Jeremiah 13:10). But they were still God's people, and Jeremiah could not bear to see them destroyed. Jeremiah said,

> If you will not listen,
>   my soul will weep in secret...;

> my eyes will weep bitterly and run down with tears,
> because the LORD's flock has been taken captive.
>
> (Jeremiah 13:17)

If Jeremiah loved the people that much, God loved them even more. And God's desire was not to crush his people but to redeem them. The Exile was their punishment, but what was the next step? What could God do to get the people to be true to the covenant? This dilemma led to the idea of the new covenant.

WORDS FOR OUR TIME

Jeremiah's "new covenant" passage is one of the truly great passages of the Old Testament. In it Jeremiah shows a depth of understanding and a sensitivity of spirit that few have matched, either before or since. As Christians, we are people of the new covenant; and there are several things about this new covenant that we should not miss.

Notice first that the covenant is not new in terms of its purpose. God's purpose remains the same—to mold the people of Israel into the people of God. The covenant is not new in terms of its wording. That too remains the same: "I will be their God, and they shall be my people" (Jeremiah 31:33). In addition, the newness of the covenant is not to be found in its content. The law that the people are to obey is the same law they had from the beginning.

The newness of the new covenant lies in God's new strategy. The fatal flaw of the old covenant was that it was external, written on stone (Exodus 34:27-28). Writing the old covenant on tablets of stone enabled the people to know what God's laws were but did not give the people the incentive to live by them. As a result, the people resisted the laws, ignored them, and tried to circumvent them. The new covenant, by contrast, will be *internal*, written "on their hearts." God's laws, rather than being imposed from without, will well up from within. And obedience to these laws will no longer be a matter of outward conformity but a matter of inward desire. People will obey God's laws because God's will has now become their will and God's purposes their purposes.

However, that is not all. When the new covenant comes into being, all the people will know God, "from the least of them to the greatest" (Jeremiah 31:34). The people will no longer need to teach their neighbors about God, for "they shall all know me," says the Lord (verse 34). God's law will be written on all their hearts.

And notice, finally, that the new covenant is made possible because

God in his grace will forgive the people and "remember their sin no more" (verse 34). Were the guilt of past sins not erased from their hearts, the people could not bear to have God's law written there. It is only as their sins are forgiven that they are free to enter into a new covenant. And so it is with us.

WORDS FOR MY LIFE

The writers of the New Testament proclaim that in Christ Jesus the new covenant has become a reality. Christians no longer serve "under the old written code," said Paul, but serve rather "in the new life of the Spirit" (Romans 7:6). Jeremiah had promised that God would write the law on the hearts of his people, but God did something even better than that. He "sent the Spirit of his Son into our hearts" (Galatians 4:6). We therefore are "discharged from the law" (Romans 7:6) and live by the Spirit. Since "God's love has been poured into our hearts through the Holy Spirit" (Romans 5:5), we are no longer "slaves of sin" (Romans 6:17). We have been given both the incentive and the power to be "obedient from the heart" (Romans 6:17).

However, we know that we are not always obedient. Sin still has a powerful grip on us. If we are "set free from sin" (Romans 6:18), we do not exercise that freedom. And if we are "dead to that which held us captive" (Romans 7:6), we do not demonstrate it. The question of "why" haunts us. What is the problem? Is the new covenant no more effective than the old? Will the Christian church be no better than ancient Israel in fulfilling God's purpose in the world?

That issue brings us to an important point. You and I know that there are many promises made in the Old Testament about what God will do in the future. We know too that many of these promises were fulfilled with the coming of Jesus Christ. But let us not overlook the fact that quite frequently these promises were so far-reaching in their import that even today their complete fulfillment still lies in the future. Thus it is with this great promise of the new covenant. The new covenant is here, but we have not yet appropriated all its characteristics. We are "being transformed into [Christ's] image" (2 Corinthians 3:18), but we are not there yet. Our obedience is still not perfect. Our hearts are not yet pure. The church is not yet "holy and without blemish" (Ephesians 5:27). Nevertheless, we are the people of the new covenant. God has put his Spirit within us and has written his law on our hearts.

"The days are surely coming, says the LORD, when I will make a new covenant with the house of Israel." For you and me, that day is here.

13
LET JUSTICE ROLL

Amos 5:21-24

Let justice roll down like waters,
and righteousness like an ever-flowing stream.
Amos 5:24

WORDS FOR BIBLE TIMES

This foreigner was claiming to speak for God:

I hate, I despise your festivals,
and I take no delight in your solemn assemblies.
(Amos 5:21)

Amos had come north from the neighboring kingdom of Judah. He stood near the altar at Bethel where the king of Israel worshiped.

Listening were those who had come to the royal altar to participate in the very practices that this stranger was denouncing. The foreigner's words struck the people like an unprovoked slap in the face. Amos went further: God did not want their burnt offerings, their cereal offerings, or their peace offerings. None of these were acceptable to the Almighty. The people's songs and the music of their harps were just offensive noise to God.

Despite the protests of the priest at Bethel, Amos detailed the total destruction that God would bring upon the people of Israel. Their prized achievements, possessions, and lavish homes were going to be destroyed, Amos told them. Their nation would be crushed. The people would be scattered and subjected to terrible suffering.

They had ignored God's repeated warnings, Amos reminded them. They had refused many opportunities to turn from their sinfulness. Now, the prophet said, the days of their punishment had arrived. Only after all the sinners were destroyed would the nation be restored.

However, the people of Israel liked things the way they were. The rich enjoyed their fine houses of stone and their beds of ivory. They valued the long period of peace and prosperity they were enjoying. If the poor were treated badly, who cared? If they were sold into slavery when they were unable to repay a small debt, who cared? If sabbath hours and feast days were shortened so places of business could stay open longer, who cared? If Israel adopted some of the festivals and practices of its pagan neighbors, who cared? After all, the Israelites kept the feasts and made the sacrifices God expected.

Yet God's answer was clear, Amos said:

> Let justice roll down like waters,
>   and righteousness like an ever-flowing stream.
>
>   (Amos 5:24)

WORDS FOR OUR TIME

You and I know that justice does not flow freely as water through our land. Righteousness does not gush forth like a living stream. We know that all too often the kind of justice people receive depends on the kind of lawyer they can afford, the connections they have with persons of power, and a number of other factors. Guilt or innocence is a minor issue in many cases.

Not only is there crime in the dark streets and alleys, there is deliberate deception and wrongdoing by persons in positions of trust. Although we may attempt to make ourselves secure behind dead bolts, burglar alarms, and guard dogs, the exaggerated claims and misrepresentations of advertising enter our homes through the media and victimize us through "acceptable" means of fraud.

The prophet's vision of what truly pleases God is as refreshing to contemplate in our time as it was in the centuries before Jesus walked this earth. How wonderful it would be to live in a society in which every person could expect justice. How delightful it would be if each person we encountered had an overpowering desire to do what was good and right in every situation. The prophet's dream is surely attractive and relevant in our time.

However, like the prophet, we know all too well that trickery, deceit, dishonesty, and exploitation are everywhere. We recognize also that some of the worst offenders brazenly offer eloquent prayers, make impressive contributions to charity, and place themselves among the pious members of the community.

Phony expressions of piety and insincere offerings by those who exploit the weak, crush all opposition to injustice, and use any means to get what they want are sickening to us. With the prophet we must ask what joy God could find in such deceit-riddled offerings. False expressions of worship are as repulsive today as they were when Amos observed them.

We all know the empty feeling we experience when people flatter us and we realize they are insincere. How much more offensive it must be to God when eloquent expressions of praise are sounded and conspicuous offerings of funds are made by those whom God knows to be concealing hearts of cruelty, arrogance, and evil.

WORDS FOR MY LIFE

It is difficult to avoid remembering Jesus' words at this point: "Let anyone among you who is without sin be the first to throw a stone" (John 8:7). Am I so different from the other members of my community that the conditions I have deplored in it have no existence in my own life and actions? Am I wholly without guilt or deception? Is there no greed or lust for power in my heart? Do I truly seek and desire impartial justice in every situation? Are my efforts at all times exerted to support righteousness, whatever the effects may be on me or on those I love most?

My inclination is to slink away, leaving such questions unanswered. However, I know that the same words that condemned the practices of the people in Amos's day also condemn me. The deceit, the lusts, the greed, and the arrogance that I deplore are also in me. Bitter as the recognition may be, I must acknowledge that I share in the guilt. I help make our times the way they are. Although I may not have actively created some of the conditions, I have allowed or supported them for reasons of my own. Perhaps I did not care enough to do anything about what I knew was wrong or unjust. Possibly I was afraid of what would happen to me or to others who are important in my life if I opposed an unjust situation. Maybe I just did not give it much thought. Whatever the reason, my passivity served to allow the evil, injustice, and wrong to stand unchallenged and to increase. Amos's condemnation is inescapable; it is addressed to me too.

The prophet's words strike deep into any heart and soul. Do my acts of worship and my sacrificial gifts find favor in God's sight? What if my acts of worship are acts of habit rather than acts of praise? If that is the case, how does God receive my expressions of thankfulness? If my heart is cold and insensitive to the needs of my suffering neighbors or if I give to charity because someone important to me will know I have done so, then how can God view my offerings in any way except with contempt?

I must acknowledge that there is not always contrition in my heart when I join others in prayers asking God's forgiveness. There is not always praise in my heart when I join in singing hymns of praise. I am not always filled with thankfulness when I comply with a request to offer thanks to God for this or that. Is it otherwise with you? Amos's words make me feel more than a little uncomfortable, and they should.

14
THE BEATITUDES

Matthew 5:1-12

Blessed are the poor in spirit, for theirs is the kingdom of heaven.
Blessed are those who mourn, for they will be comforted.
Blessed are the meek, for they will inherit the earth.
Blessed are those who hunger and thirst for righteousness, for they will be filled.
Blessed are the merciful, for they will receive mercy.
Blessed are the pure in heart, for they will see God.
Blessed are the peacemakers, for they will be called children of God.
Blessed are those who are persecuted for righteousness' sake, for theirs is the kingdom of heaven.
Blessed are you when people revile you and persecute you and utter all kinds of evil against you falsely on my account. Rejoice and be glad, for your reward is great in heaven, for in the same way they persecuted the prophets who were before you.　　　　　　Matthew 5:3-12

WORDS FOR BIBLE TIMES

There was excitement in Israel. A wonderworker had appeared. He could heal any illness instantly. He could restore sight to the blind. He could outwit the most clever leaders. When he was present, a bit of food could be turned into enough to feed a large crowd. At his command evil spirits fled and dead persons returned to life. People could be miraculously restored to health just by coming close to him. And his stories of the new kingdom were thrilling to hear.

People began to gather early in the day. They came from every direction. From Tyre and Sidon in the north and from Jerusalem in the south, the people came. Eyes eager with anticipation, they looked for Jesus. They had heard that Jesus and his closest companions could often be seen walking along the north shore of the Sea of Galilee.

As Jesus and his disciples approached, he saw the crowd at a distance. He knew what the people wanted. Some came seeking a personal benefit—a miraculous cure, an expulsion of evil spirits, or a bit of advice. A few were there to try to trick him into some statement or action that would cause him to have trouble with the authorities. Some had come to learn more about the kingdom he described. And many came to see a show, whether that be the performing of a miracle or the matching of wits with questioners.

The size of the crowd that had gathered alarmed Jesus' opponents. Without question, Jesus' popularity was increasing. Those who opposed Jesus feared that soon the whole nation would be following him. Jesus' opponents intended to keep that from happening.

Maybe their opportunity would come during the day. They imagined how Jesus would glow with pride at the size of the audience he was able to attract. They hoped that in this moment of pride he might relax. That instant when his thoughts and speech were unguarded would be their opportunity. If they could trick him into saying or doing something that could be interpreted as blasphemy or that was contrary to the law in some way, they might be able to lessen his influence.

However, Jesus' actions surprised everyone, including his opponents. Matthew 5:1 tells us that Jesus left the crowds behind and led a few persons to a mountaintop. (Matthew 7:28, however, says that at the end of the Sermon on the Mount, "the crowds were astounded at his teaching." The words of the sermon, especially the opening Beatitudes, surely are appropriate for all who would follow Christ, not just for special disciples.)

In the usual style of a rabbi of that day, Jesus probably sat down; and his disciples gathered around him to hear his teaching. In a few brief sentences Jesus outlined a new understanding of who should be considered favored or blessed by God and of who it is who has a place in the kingdom of heaven. As in much of his teaching, Jesus' statements seemed to be directly contrary to the prevailing views of his time. It is little wonder that his teachings enraged the leaders of Judea and increased their opposition to him and his ministry.

WORDS FOR OUR TIME

The Beatitudes are as relevant and valuable in our time as they were in the days of the apostles. Unfortunately, people today are just as blind to what Jesus taught in these statements as the apostles were before they learned to see things differently.

In Matthew's Gospel, Jesus' first beatitude is "Blessed are the poor in spirit." According to Luke 6:20, Jesus said "Blessed are you who are poor." He may have made both statements on separate occasions. In either case the statement is certainly as baffling in our time as it was in the first century. To be poor in spirit is to be lacking in power, influence, and material possessions. There can be little difference between being poor in spirit and simply being poor. How could being poor result in being blessed? What makes poverty a happy and God-favored condition?

The "superstar," the conquering hero, and persons with enormous power and possessions are the people who are envied and imitated in our time. The poor, the weak, the less assertive, and compliant persons and groups are those who tend to be ignored, pushed around, and considered to have little potential. The winner, not the loser, is valued today. If the lives of the losers are wasted, who cares?

Even in the churches more attention is often paid to affluent community leaders than to persons of lower social status. However, God is not awed by the possessions and achievements of anyone. Each human being is God's creation. There is an equal place for each of us in the household of God. Now, as then, Jesus opens the Kingdom to all who will enter. Surprisingly, those who feel most worthless and downtrodden, persecuted and hopeless, are the very ones who are most intensely blessed.

Persons who feel impoverished in their spiritual life are the ones who accept most eagerly the riches of the kingdom of heaven. It is those who are mourning who are most ready for the comfort and strength God offers. The meek, who "come in last" to take what is left after the aggressive have grabbed what they want, are not ruled out. The meek are especially open to the invitation to become the good stewards of God's creation. And it is those who hunger and thirst for righteousness who are most readily drawn into the Kingdom in which righteousness is everywhere in evidence.

Jesus taught that the Kingdom is for the good of each of us. The Kingdom is best for those who need it most. The kingdom of God is for those who can value it and appreciate it and live joyously with what it offers. The merciful, the pure in heart, workers for peace, and the unjustly persecuted can understand and appreciate what the Kingdom offers. These are the persons whom God favors in our time as in ages past.

WORDS FOR MY LIFE

It is a pleasure to watch a group of youngsters rush to the dinner table after a period of vigorous athletic competition. They are famished, and everything looks and tastes great. There is no need for begging, cajoling, or tricking them into eating foods that are "good for them."

Perhaps God has a somewhat similar enjoyment in seeing ethically and spiritually famished persons enjoy the blessings of the kingdom of heaven as they become aware of their freedom and their ability to enjoy these blessings.

By comparison, how baffling it must be to those who are experiencing the happiness of God's favor to watch others, who have no awareness of the Kingdom, as they struggle and squabble about matters of little ultimate significance. How foolish it must seem to God when we attach great importance to which of us holds the higher title in the organization, which of us drives the more expensive car, which of us is dressed in the latest fashion, or which of us has the most "admirable" ancestry.

Proudly as we may strut, we can never approach a level of achievement or a quantity of possession that would demand God's favor. God's favor is an unearned gift. With this fact in mind, we must recognize that the Beatitudes do not constitute a set of goals for us to achieve in order to win the favor of God. Instead, they point out to us how little our possessions, our achievements, and our public approval have to do with receiving God's favor.

Through Christ, our eyes and minds and hearts are opened. We begin to see what is really going on in ourselves and in the world around us. God did not depart from the world after creating it. God continues to be with us. God did not turn control of this world over to any king, nation, or assemblage. God is our judge and ruler yet. To live for any goal other than those God commends is futile and foolish.

Jesus described the demand that is placed on each of us. If I am to live within God's favor, I must love God with my whole being and love my neighbor as well as myself.

Unfortunately, my pride, ambition, and greed—my lust for honor, power, and possessions—can blind me to the needs and sufferings of my fellow human beings. Selfish concerns can also cause me to forget my relationship with God and my dependence on him. So, I am tempted to block myself out of God's favor and to live as if I were a citizen of an alien kingdom. I live this way even though God's rule is more encompassing and enduring than any human kingdom. However, God continues to offer me the opportunity to have that enduring relationship Christians call "love divine, all loves excelling."

15
I WILL GIVE YOU REST

Rules for Jesus'
Exodus
Lev'
Numbers

2/3 of verses
Luke, Math
Mark

Matthew 11:28-30
Taken all teaching
as how people are to act

Come to me, all you that are weary and are carrying heavy burdens, and I will give you rest. Take my yoke upon you, and learn from me; for I am gentle and humble in heart, and you will find rest for your souls. For my yoke is easy, and my burden is light.
Matthew 11:28-30

WORDS FOR BIBLE TIMES

The sky was dark. The day was not going well. Jesus was disappointed. He had spent weeks doing mighty works near the Sea of Galilee. Jesus had expected those who watched and listened to repent of their evil ways. He had told them how God wanted them to live. Now he felt like condemning them. "Just wait," he said to them. "You will be punished for ignoring what I have told you. Chorazin, Bethsaida, and Capernaum," Jesus named three towns from which his hearers had just come, "your fate will be worse than that of Sodom, which God utterly destroyed. Just wait!" (see Matthew 11:20-24).

However, condemning the cities did not solve the problem. Jesus thought of the resistance he was getting from important leaders. The persons who were most educated and most powerful seemed to be against him. Yet they were expecting the Messiah. Where was he failing?

The worst blow of all had come from John the Baptist. He had sent representatives to ask Jesus if he really was the Messiah (Matthew 11:2-3). Was the person who had first pointed to Jesus as the Messiah (Matthew 3:13-17) beginning to have doubts? Jesus sent back a crisp response, simply listing his wondrous works. John could form his own judgments. Who except the Messiah could do such things (Matthew 11:4-6)?

How interesting that after confronting John's doubts (verses 2-5) and responding sharply to indifferent witnesses (verses 20-23), Jesus thanked God for hiding truth from the wise and revealing it to the simple (verse 25).

Jesus' prayer indicates that he now understands clearly. The common people, those who make no pretense of being wise, hear him gladly. He will teach them. They will learn that to do as God wants is much less burdensome than to do all that the "important" people demand.

At that point Matthew includes the beautiful invitation Jesus offered: "Come...take my yoke...learn...find rest." The invitation seems to be modeled on the closing passage in the apocryphal book called Ecclesiasticus (51:23-27):

> Draw near to me, you who are uneducated....
> Put your neck under her yoke,
>   and let your souls receive instruction....
> See with your own eyes that I have labored but little
>   and found for myself much serenity.

The response of the common people to Jesus' invitation has planted seeds of change across the world.

WORDS FOR OUR TIME

Jesus' invitation is attractive in our time, just as it was in Bible times. However, we often hear only the first part of the invitation—the offer of rest. We tend to overlook the heart of the matter.

Jesus did not describe a condition of relaxed, passive goodness as God's intended goal for human beings. Instead, Jesus advocated active demonstrations of love.

As a carpenter, Jesus would have known that there were great differences in yokes. Some of these yokes were so smoothly carved and so well-fitted to the necks of work animals that heavy loads could be pulled without pain to the animals. Other yokes were roughly constructed and poorly fitted. The oxen's skin and flesh were rubbed raw. But whether the yoke was comfortable or almost unendurable, its purpose was to help get work done.

The promise in Jesus' invitation is not that his followers can avoid work. He offers a means of doing our tasks that will not overly tax our endurance or cause pain that could have been avoided. Christ will help us accomplish the work to which he calls us.

Jesus Christ offers to teach us the work God would have us do. What is this work?

• eliminating the systems of injustice and the practices of unrighteousness that make life difficult and joyless for so many of our fellow human beings;

• showing our appreciation for God's creativity by exercising responsible stewardship of everything God has created;

• expressing love in every relationship with other human beings rather than exploiting them, humiliating them, or making their lives less fulfilling in any way;

• caring for the minds, hearts, souls, and bodies that God has given us.

In his life, his words, and his works, Jesus gave us the benefit of his understanding of God and of God's will for us. We can accept Jesus' invitation gladly and learn from him. It is offered by one who is gentle and who knows our needs and problems as well as we do. It is offered by one who knows the answers and resources available to help us do God's will. Jesus Christ assures us that our lives will not be burdensome and exhausting but refreshing and restful when we follow him.

However, the choice to follow Jesus is ours. We can do as some of the learned, powerful people did in the first century: resist, reject, or ignore what he is offering to teach us.

WORDS FOR MY LIFE

At the end of a week of hard labor, it is so easy to relax in a comfortable church pew. I sing praises to God. I listen to inspiring prayers, Scripture readings, sermons, and other parts of the church's rituals. There, when it is so easy and so enjoyable, I can think of all the promises Jesus and his followers have made to those who accept him as Lord. I can congratulate myself on having been led to Christ by kind and wonderful Christians and having been sustained by a loving congregation.

From the teachings of Jesus and from other writings in the Bible, I can have my heart and mind filled with inspiring, uplifting, and encouraging words. I can find assurances of a glorious future for myself and for those I love most. Peace fills my whole being as I experience the marvelous resources of the Christian faith.

But I cannot stop there. The worship service is just the resting time of the week. Beyond the worship is the work that makes me ready for the resting time again.

What more would Jesus teach me that God desires and expects from me? Have I considered the growing number of homeless persons? They are trying to survive by living in packing boxes, under bridges, or simply on the streets. I live in a comfortable home and have ample food, clothing, and other necessities. God, who created us all and loves us all equally, cannot be pleased with such inequity. God expects me to help the homeless. This problem is of such magnitude and complexity that I cannot solve it alone. I need to join hands and mind and heart with other persons who are trying to solve this problem. Jesus has invited us to learn from him. As we learn, we must feel the yoke on our shoulders to work at correcting this intolerable situation.

Other problems exist that I as a follower of Christ must address. I am obligated to learn what these problems are and how to deal with them.

A full week's work waits for me before I am ready to enjoy the restful and private renewal of my strength, my faith, and my appreciation of God's creation. I need the work, and I need the rest.

My efforts are voluntary, however. God does not put the yoke on me without my consent. I am invited to take it upon myself and then to learn from Christ how to carry out my tasks.

Children - Love them, proud of them
Stop saying what they do wrong
Tell them they are the best at
(whatever they do best)

16
THE LEAST OF THESE

Matthew 25:31-46

Truly I tell you, just as you did it to one of the least of these who are members of my family, you did it to me.   Matthew 25:40

WORDS FOR BIBLE TIMES

Like a group of high-powered corporate executives, the religious officials challenged Jesus as he arrived at the Temple (Matthew 21:23). He tried to point out problems and defects in the system they were managing. These defects were so glaring they seemed self-evident. Jesus vividly described one problem after another. Surely the leaders could see the need to correct such faults. Surely some of them would recognize and appreciate his efforts to improve what they were doing.

However, the religious leaders did not receive Jesus with appreciation. All day long they rejected his insights, contested his observations, and disputed his conclusions. They refused to accept anything he said. There was no point in trying further. Jesus ended the conversation with a question they did not dare answer (Matthew 22:41-46). There was silence. Then Jesus turned to the crowds and to his disciples and gave a scathing denunciation of these leaders, calling them blind guides and hypocrites (Matthew 23:13-33).

Then Jesus and his disciples left the Temple and went across the valley to the Mount of Olives to plan for their Passover feast. As the disciples sought further understanding (Matthew 24:3), Jesus told them parables and prophecies and shared with them interpretations of Scripture and other insights.

One parable, about the Last Judgment, must have shocked the disciples. In it Jesus identified himself completely with the poor, the suffering, and the lonely. He said whatever was done or not done to these persons was done or not done to him.

WORDS FOR OUR TIME

Jesus' parable of the Last Judgment is almost "too hot" for us to handle. It forces us to think in a way that is nearly the opposite of our usual way.

In our time we like to think of Jesus as the perfect, spotless, saintly being who is the model of everything we regard as good. On the other hand, we tend to feel revulsion at the thought of close association with murderers, rapists, thieves, and child abusers. We shrink from direct contact with persons with AIDS. We even hesitate to approach people who live in poverty.

To see Jesus in each of these persons can be quite difficult for some of us. But it was also hard to do when Jesus spoke the words of this parable.

The point of the parable is unmistakably clear, however. Whatever we do to the person our society values least is what we are doing to Jesus. And what we neglect doing to such a person is what we are neglecting to do to Jesus. There is no other interpretation.

In our time a few people do accept the truth in this parable. They do not attempt to shield themselves from contact with other human beings. They share the anxieties, the sufferings, and the heartbreaks of those who are least acceptable in our society.

Those of us who have not experienced such associations think of "the few" as saints. But they assure us that we are mistaken. They are simply helping fellow human beings—God's creatures like themselves—whom God loves as fully as he loves us. These persons are simply obeying the commandment to love our neighbor as we love ourselves.

Most of us search for a compromise position from which to work. Knowing that we "freeze up," paralyzed by negative emotions when we try to relate directly to those we have learned to fear and avoid, we try to discover a comfortable limit to how far we can go. Nearly all of us find that we can go far enough to send something. We can send money. We can send workers who are willing to go as our representatives. We can send supplies that may be needed or helpful.

But we also need to consider what we receive from the "least of these," to whom we are willing to send. Perhaps we receive only negative "vibrations." When that is the case, we need to work at seeing the so-called social misfits as God's creation—as Jesus Christ's brothers and sisters—as our brothers and sisters. Then perhaps we can know their sufferings and feel a greater readiness to help these people and to get to know them. Those whom we call saints are unanimous in acknowledging that they personally benefit from friendships with "the least, the last, and the lost."

WORDS FOR MY LIFE

When I think of this shocking parable in terms of my personal life, I have two strong feelings. The first is a feeling of profound guilt. Not only do I fear and want to avoid persons whom our society rejects, I have also taught my children to value cleanliness and neatness, to avoid bad influences, and to concentrate on making something "worthwhile" of their lives. Although I may not have been as successful in these teachings as I wanted to be, I can see evidence in my children's lives that they did assimilate some of that influence. While I would still affirm the value of what I tried to teach, my feeling of guilt comes from the realization that I may also have taught my children to scorn persons to whom cleanliness and neatness are not top priorities. (Only the homeless can know how difficult it can be to stay neat and clean.)

The other feeling is that of regret. I regret that I have not actively pursued the opportunities that have come to me from time to time to know individuals personally whom I now might fear or avoid. When I was a ministerial student, I worked and lived in the slums of a large city. A cherished memory of my first day on the job is of a little two-year-old child, long unbathed and clothed in a tattered old rag. She had grimy hands and an unwiped nose. She climbed up into my lap as I sat on a low step, and I gave her a little hug. The hug she gave in response nearly strangled me, but we both knew that we had met another person and been fully accepted. Today I would not dare to enter that neighborhood without an escort. Yet I imagine that every person in that neighborhood was once a lovable little child like the one I met years ago and that the person in them is as real as the person in me.

Unquestionable is the message that comes through from Jesus' parable of the Last Judgment. If we are to lead a Christian life, we cannot live behind impenetrable shields that isolate us from other human beings. We have to risk living with one another. We have to be vulnerable and perhaps lose our health, our life, or our financial resources in the process. We have to get close enough to feel the person who is inside all the repulsive trappings that we see from a distance. We have to get close enough to know the pain that the other person is experiencing and close enough to know what would help to ease that suffering.

Terrified as we often are of each other, Jesus insists that we meet each other honestly, helpfully, and lovingly in whatever circumstances either of us finds ourself. We must live this way if we are to meet him also as our Lord and brother.

17
GO INTO ALL THE WORLD

Matthew 28:16-20

All authority in heaven and on earth has been given to me. Go therefore and make disciples of all nations, baptizing them in the name of the Father and of the Son and of the Holy Spirit, and teaching them to obey everything that I have commanded you. And remember, I am with you always, to the end of the age.

Matthew 28:18-20

WORDS FOR BIBLE TIMES

When the Gospel of Matthew was written, more than sixty years had passed since Jesus walked among and talked with the people. No longer could persons be found who had had direct contact with the Messiah. A few people had put into writing collections of Jesus' sayings on various subjects. And a few of the churches cherished letters from people who said they had known Jesus personally. However, the slow task of copying such documents by hand meant that few copies were made. Most of the churches had to rely on memories of what various persons had heard from others, who in turn had received their information indirectly.

The writer of Matthew apparently realized that the early Christians needed a book to guide them in their life and work together. Lack of detailed guidance had produced much divisiveness and false teaching in the churches. There were many questions that no one could answer.

Each congregation had been struggling with difficult questions such as
• Who was Christ, and where did he come from? (Some said he was a spirit who had come to earth from heaven for a brief period. Others said he was a man whose coming the Jewish prophets had predicted.)
• By what authority were Christians to decide whether to follow the teachings of Jesus or the Jewish law when there were significant differences between them? (Some said Jesus received guidance directly from God. Others argued that Jesus simply interpreted the law differently from earlier rabbis.)
• What is the proper thing to say when baptizing someone. (Some said, "In the name of Jesus." Others felt that God and the Holy Spirit should also be mentioned.)
• How should people understand the meaning of the Lord's Supper?
• Should Christians allow or invite members of other religions to become Christians?

These and multitudes of comparable questions created problems and divisiveness in the churches.

At this point in history the writer of Matthew drew together many collections of Jesus' sayings, reports of actions, and other remembrances about Jesus. The writer arranged them in the chronological order of a biography and provided answers to many questions that were troubling the churches.

In a sort of summary, this book, the Gospel According to Matthew, makes clear the absolute authority of Jesus and his mandate to his disciples to lead all persons everywhere to follow him. The command to teach everyone to observe a correct formula for Christian baptism closes with the assurance of Jesus' presence with his followers until the end of time.

This clear mandate to bring the whole world to Christ has been a powerful motivating force in the church for twenty centuries.

WORDS FOR OUR TIME

The authority of Christians to seek to convert members of other religions to the Christian faith has been a matter of controversy in recent years. Many nations have closed their borders to those who would enter for that purpose. Church leaders have questioned the propriety of attempting evangelism in defiance of restrictions by these countries. Many missionaries today see their task as fostering international dialogue. They express their Christian faith through humanitarian aid and actions for social improvement rather than through direct attempts at evangelism.

Some nations have tried to block almost any effort to increase the number of adherents to the Christian faith in their lands. However, in other nations some restrictions have been loosened, and efforts to spread the Christian faith have increased proportionately.

Ironically, the situation in America seems to be moving in the opposite direction. Because of the increasing pluralism in religion in the United States, there is growing resistance to allowing Christianity a favored status.

Can Christians be satisfied with interfaith dialogue, political debate and action, and multifaith humanitarian efforts as the church's primary involvement in American life? If so, how am I to make disciples and to teach all that Jesus Christ commands?

WORDS FOR MY LIFE

A bitter truth that I hate to acknowledge is that some of the greatest advances in Christianity have come in times of greatest hardship, controversy, and suffering in the community of Christians. Most of us have grown up in a land where our faith is widely shared and seldom questioned in any threatening manner. As a result, we have become lax and somewhat careless about the preservation and maintenance of our religious heritage.

The Old Testament is full of examples of God's people neglecting their faith and forgetting their responsibilities during times of ease and affluence. Are we just one more example in this historic array?

I do not like to think of having to fight for my right to be a Christian. But that is what many of our sisters and brothers in the faith have to face. It is saddening to think of being unable to speak freely to others of the joys and fulfillments of my life as a Christian. But that is the present condition of many people. It is dismaying to think of having to justify and defend the authority given to me and to you in Matthew 28:18-20 to help others become Christians. But we would not be the first to struggle with that problem.

We in the United States are not yet at the point of having to establish our rights as members of a minority faith group. We should appreciate our religious freedom, and we need to ask seriously how we may best use this freedom.

Most of us will not be in other lands for extended periods of time or with any great frequency. Therefore, we need to focus our attention on our opportunities for evangelism in the communities where we live and work.

We share the Great Commission to make disciples of all people. What have we done this week to fulfill that responsibility? We have met and dealt with dozens, perhaps hundreds, of persons in this brief period. What holds us back from talking with them about our faith? We have discussed our political preferences, our favorite sports figures, our opinions of the weather, our feelings about reported misdeeds of elected officials, our views on crime and our justice system. Why not our faith?

Most of us find it easy to encourage people to make a commitment to Christ in gatherings identified as "religious" or sponsored by the church. But we seem by mutual agreement to avoid such topics in other settings. Why? Sometimes we know the religious affiliation of the other person and simply want to avoid getting embroiled in a nonproductive argument. Sometimes we try not to offend another person by challenging the adequacy of his or her religious faith. But nothing really absolves us of our responsibility. As disciples, we are to find ways to take the initiative. Jesus said, "Go." Let's get started.

18
JESUS BEGINS HIS MISSION

Mark 1:4-20

Jesus came to Galilee, proclaiming the good news of God, and saying, "The time is fulfilled, and the kingdom of God has come near; repent, and believe in the good news."

Mark 1:14-15

WORDS FOR BIBLE TIMES

"Elijah has returned! The prophet is here!" The news swept through the land. People hurried to see for themselves.

The return of Elijah was an event the Jewish people had been expecting for a long time. The prophet Malachi had said that God would send Elijah to warn the people just before the terrible Day of Judgment (Malachi 4:5).

At the edge of the desert east of Jerusalem, the people gathered. Standing beside the Jordan River, the prophet was an awesome sight. His name was John. But his appearance was the same as the description of Elijah (2 Kings 1:8). John had appeared near the spot where, according to tradition, Elijah had been taken up in a whirlwind (2 Kings 2:11).

The voice of the prophet was strong and confident: "Turn from your evil ways! Turn to God! The terrible day of God's judgment is arriving!" Urgently John described the coming judgment and the punishment awaiting those who refused to heed the warning and to turn to God.

Many people waded into the river. Jesus was among those who responded to the prophet's words.

As Jesus came up out of the water, he experienced an affirmation of himself such as he had never felt before. He knew now that he was loved by God, as God's Son. And God was pleased with him. At this point, Jesus needed to fast and pray and think. So he went alone into the desert wilderness. At the end of forty days he was ready.

Returning to Galilee, Jesus began to preach. His message was not quite the same as that which John had been preaching by the Jordan. John by this time had been arrested and imprisoned (Mark 1:14). John had preached about the sinfulness of the people and about the coming Day of Judgment and its terrors. Jesus preached about the glorious kingdom of justice, righteousness, and love that God was establishing. Jesus offered the Kingdom to those who were willing to turn from their worldly concerns and to become God's people.

While walking beside the beautiful Sea of Galilee one day, Jesus saw some fishermen. He talked with them. They discussed the work he was doing. He invited these men to share in it as his disciples. They responded readily, accepting this challenge and leaving their old lives behind them.

With his little band of four disciples—Simon Peter, Andrew, James, and John—Jesus entered the city of Capernaum, where he began to teach and heal. However, most people had little understanding of the importance and meaning of what was happening in their midst. Their daily routines, problems, and joys commanded all their attention and energy.

WORDS FOR OUR TIME

The offer of God's kingdom is as attractive today as it was in Jesus' time. Every nation in the world needs to come under the influence of God's rule.

Unfortunately, our selfish interests and concerns control us. We devote our time, our energy, and our resources to earning money and to spending it. We exhaust ourselves and others in our struggle for recognition and power. We long for luxury even though we know so many people have no hope of having the basic necessities of life. And we give at least our tacit support to systems of injustice, oppression, and cruelty.

Jesus said: "The time is fulfilled, and the kingdom of God has come near" (Mark 1:15). This news is good indeed. Our time is one of readiness for change. Many people feel that we are at the beginning of a new era. No one has a clear sense of what the new era is going to be like, but people feel certain that it is going to be different from the present world order. Our nation, like all other nations, is deeply troubled. We want and need a better society. We yearn for a society in which we can trust one another. We yearn for a society in which love, justice, and righteousness permeate all that we do and say.

Jesus called for repentance. We have offered penitence. But that is not enough. Repentance is what is required. Repentance is not just the emotional regret and sorrow for what we have done wrong or allowed to happen—that is penitence. Repentance is the actual turning from the evil we are doing, from the idols we are serving, such as wealth, power, and prestige. Repentance is not just deciding to turn, as in a "New Year's resolution." It is actually turning to God as the only master we serve. Repenting means devoting our time and energy to following God's ways. Nothing less can cure the sickness of human society.

WORDS FOR MY LIFE

If society as a whole cannot comprehend or obey a call for repentance, individuals find it just as difficult. Whether rich or poor, privileged or underprivileged, most of us have worked out a way of living that provides us with some degree of satisfaction. We have "learned the rules" by which "the game is played." Whether we call it being "street wise" or sophisticated or well-adjusted, we have learned how to "make it" in our world. Unpleasant, degrading, and unsatisfactory as our way of life may be, we tend to resist giving it up and entering a new world in which we have no experience.

A person must have courage to become an immigrant—even an immigrant to the kingdom of God. Learning anew how to "see" things, how to behave, even how to communicate, can be a terrifying experience. Yet we know that this process is part of what is involved when we say yes to the Kingdom. When we respond positively to Jesus' invitation to repent, we must turn from our present ways to God's ways.

But when immigrants cross into this bold new kingdom, they must have determination to remain. Whatever its inadequacies, "home" exerts a powerful pull on the heart-strings. After spending time among people who speak differently, think differently, act differently, and feel differently, we are tempted to return home where we feel at ease. To repent is to turn. Unfortunately, to turn a second time is also tempting.

Yes, Jesus' call strikes a responsive chord in my heart. I yearn for a society in which love, justice, and righteousness are everywhere. And I feel that the time is long overdue for the rule of God. I firmly believe that Jesus Christ reveals the true nature of God and God's will. Christ offers the desired Kingdom to us. All this comes rather easily. But it is not as easy to free myself from the world in which I feel so much at home.

I value some of my possessions in a special way. I truly cherish them. Some of my relationships with other persons are particularly meaningful to me. As a result, I make a special effort to spend time with these people. I have organized my life around certain goals. I feel a deep sense of fulfillment when I achieve them. I like that feeling.

Does responding positively to Jesus' call to repentance mean that I must turn from all these valued parts of my present world when I turn to God? If so, I cannot do it alone. I need some help. Perhaps this is one of the important functions of the church—to help persons like me who love our world too dearly to turn loose of it. I want to live in God's realm of justice, righteousness, and love. I need those loving friends I find in the church to help my faltering steps in that direction.

19
THE BIRTH OF JESUS

Luke 1:26-56; 2:1-40

Do not be afraid; for see—I am bringing you good news of great joy for all the people: to you is born this day in the city of David a Savior, who is the Messiah, the Lord.   Luke 2:10-11

WORDS FOR BIBLE TIMES

The sharp cry of a newborn infant broke the silence of the night. A ewe lifted her head for a moment to listen, then resumed her sleep. There was stillness under the stars. No one was aware that something important had happened—no one except the little family huddled in a cave. Then to shepherds in the hills outside Bethlehem came startling moments of fear, followed by a commanding voice: "Do not be afraid."

For hundreds of years the people of Israel had awaited the promised Messiah. Ironically, he arrived almost unnoticed, a tiny baby, unannounced to any officials or to the powerful of the land.

The Messiah did not come in the way the people had expected. No parades took place—no flourishing of trumpets, no large-scale public announcement, no arrangements negotiated with the nation's officials. Understandably, the powerful and the influential members of society questioned such a messiah's credentials and eventually rejected him.

Unless God acted as these people expected, they were unwilling to recognize that God had acted at all. Throughout his ministry Jesus had to struggle against this arrogance and against this stubborn insistence that the officially established views, understandings, and procedures be followed precisely.

When Jesus was born, the people whom he had come to redeem did not notice. They were too busy doing other things. By order of the Roman emperor all persons were required to return to their family's ancestral home. A registration was the emperor's intention, but the event became an occasion for family reunions. These reunions required much time and energy from everyone involved. People who still lived in the "old home town" had to prepare for relatives who were coming there to register. The hosts had to clean the house, get the guest quarters ready, and have extra food on hand. They also had to do more marketing than usual. The travelers had to feed and care for their beasts of burden. They wanted to purchase souvenirs. They needed to replace items lost along the way and to buy gifts for their hosts. The result was long and busy hours at the merchants' booths. With these urgent matters on the people's minds, how could they be expected to think about the long-awaited Messiah? Who would have thought God would choose such a busy time to send his Son?

People in Bible times found God's ways as hard to understand as we do today. The problem was accepting the fact that God acts when and as God chooses to act; and God's decision may be just the opposite of what people expect. But we are not in command. God is.

WORDS FOR OUR TIME

The whole Christmas story, with all its meaningful details, is heart-warming and inspiring to read and to consider. We may know it all "by heart," but it is good to hear it again—to watch it acted out by young and old. It is a beautiful and deeply loved story of how our Lord came to us.

In the accounts by Matthew and Luke, the genealogies of Jesus reinforce the prophecies of Isaiah and Jeremiah. The Messiah would be a descendant of David. The genealogies establish a legal link through Joseph with that royal lineage. We are encouraged to think deeply and imaginatively as we read the descriptions of how God came among us in human form. And as we think about the way human beings like us treated this innocent babe, we can feel the tragedy of the evil and cruelty of which we are capable.

In our time the royalty of Jesus' lineage seems inconsequential. Monarchies are almost extinct. What matters now is the fact that in Jesus we see God's love for every human being, regardless of race or class or nationality.

The highest ideals known in our time, the most profound solutions to problems of living together, and the best opportunity to live in a better world all have their origins in Jesus, whose birth cry broke the stillness of a Bethlehem night twenty centuries ago. Because of him, God is known to us in our time. Because of him, communities exist in which all persons are accepted and loved. Because of him, we have the hope of entry into the kingdom of heaven. Truly, nothing is more important for our time than the birth of Jesus, which the Gospels of Matthew and Luke describe so beautifully.

WORDS FOR MY LIFE

My daily life is much like that of the people who were too busy to notice the birth of the Messiah. I seem to have so much to do and so little time in which to do it. Have you, like me, ever wondered where the time has gone?

Some people were so feverishly busy the night Jesus was born they never knew he came into the world. He lived, he taught, he died—and they never knew he existed. How different my life would be if he had never lived. To whatever extent I fail to let Jesus into my life, the loss is mine.

Like the leaders and officials of Bible times, I find myself inspecting the credentials of unfamiliar persons before I listen to the substance of their proposals. Because Jesus did not "match" the preconceived notion that Israel's leaders had of the expected Messiah, they prevented the people from hearing and considering seriously the understandings that he offered. I am guilty of the same self-imposed blindness. I want to know whose work I am exposing myself to and what the person's qualifications are before I study his or her research report or set of conclusions. In this way I screen out a lot of "trash" that might otherwise waste my limited time. However, I sometimes wonder if Jesus would be able to get through to me if he came into the world today. Would I ignore or reject him just as most people did two thousand years ago?

Because I want to be less vulnerable in my world, I avoid taking risks, physically or emotionally. I raise a barrier to keep from getting hurt. Yet maybe I need to take the risk of feeling keenly enough to care, to trust, and to relate to others on a more personal basis. Jesus' model is a powerful example. He could feel the emptiness in the lives of the people of Jerusalem. He saw that they were too busy and too self-sufficient to notice what they lacked, and he wept over the city. I need more sensitivity of this kind to what others are suffering or lacking.

In spite of my failings, however, the birth narratives are enriching to me. They feed my spirit. The Magnificat (Luke 1:46-55) is surely one of the most beautiful expressions of praise of God that I know. Mary's words arouse feelings of joy within me whenever I read them. Or consider the Benedictus (Luke 1:68-79). The courage, the faith, and the confidence Zechariah expresses in the promises of God are contagious. I feel refreshed and renewed as I read it. Similarly, the Nunc Dimittis (Luke 2:29-32) stirs me deeply. I know of no more sensitive expression of fulfillment and appreciation at the end of a worthy life than this "closing word" of the aging Simeon.

The good news of a great joy and the commanding voice saying "Do not be afraid" were not for a few shepherds only. These majestic words somehow have resounded in all the great paintings, all the magnificent music, all the Sunday school pageants about the Nativity. The good news is news of the stirring of new life from God. You and I ought to feel that stirring within our lives.

20
GOD GAVE HIS ONLY SON

John 3:1-17

For God so loved the world that he gave his only Son, so that everyone who believes in him may not perish but may have eternal life. John 3:16

WORDS FOR BIBLE TIMES

The missionary zeal of the apostles took the Christian gospel to distant places with amazing speed, partly because synagogues were already there. Since Christian teaching was based on Hebrew Scripture, the message of Christ usually received a fair hearing at first. Later, as the early Christians were being expelled from their "home bases" in the Jewish synagogues, Jesus' central message was being heard less clearly. His promise of the imminent coming of God's kingdom of love, justice, and righteousness was receiving less attention with the passing of the years. There was a lessened emphasis on mutual love and support. "Remembrances" of Jesus and his work and words were increasingly standardized recitations without the benefit of reports of firsthand experiences.

The Christian message first had been seen against Jesus' own background of Jewish life, law, and thought. But at the close of the first century, it was beginning to be viewed against the background of Gentile philosophy.

Beginning in Asia Minor, a doctrine called Gnosticism was gaining acceptance in the churches. This teaching denied that Christ had actually come in the flesh. According to the Gnostics, the material world was evil and a good God would not take on human flesh. Many of the Gnostics argued that Jesus only seemed to be human. Others believed that the divine Christ came into or upon Jesus at his baptism and departed before the Crucifixion. Christ, these theories taught, had come as God's messenger to reveal the secret of release from the body, part of the evil material world. The few who possessed this secret knowledge or *gnosis* could share it with selected others. This salvation from captivity in the flesh was seen by the Gnostics as the mission and message of the Christian church.

John thoroughly rejected Gnosticism. He presented the position that the world is God's creation. God loves the world, and it is good. Jesus was God's Son, the Word made flesh. Human beings are not saved from sin and destruction by gaining secret knowledge of how to escape from the world as the Gnostics taught. Instead, it is through belief in Christ that persons are saved.

The highly treasured verse, John 3:16, summarizes the fresh, new interpretation that John offers. He affirms God's love for the world, the gift of God's only Son, and the promise of salvation through faith in Christ. The Judgment is not some far-off event but the choice of belief or unbelief with the immediate and automatic consequences of that choice.

Most Christians today know very little about Gnostic teaching; but they know and love John's Gospel, especially John 3:16. After many years of debate, the leaders of the churches declared the Gnostic view to be heretical. The views presented in the Gospel of John were, in the main, affirmed. The crisis of identity in the churches had been effectively resolved.

WORDS FOR OUR TIME

To comprehend the depth and extent of God's love is quite difficult. It is even harder to understand that God loves every person in the world. Our relationships with others usually teach us that love is conditional. If the required conditions are met, then love is given. But if the required conditions are not met or are violated, then love is usually withdrawn. We see the bitter consequences of withdrawn love all around us. Marriages often end in divorce. Two persons who once were in love level terrible accusations against each other. Youngsters rebel against parental control, and a situation of harmony becomes one of combat. These examples are just two instances of the fact that much of the love we see and experience is conditional love. We must earn it by doing or becoming what is expected and required. If we do not "measure up," the love is withdrawn.

However, God's love is not conditional. God's love flows out freely to every person. We do not have to earn it. We do not have to feel anxious about the possibility of losing it. John tells us that God never withdraws this love, even when we human beings abuse, torture, and kill God's only Son.

We desperately need to experience this love—a love that we can scarcely comprehend. And it is so available and so easy to receive, John assures us. We have only to open ourselves to God's Spirit offered to us through Christ. Our act of belief is the response that enables us to become part of God's eternal kingdom of love.

WORDS FOR MY LIFE

Much of what we do and say and think is rooted in what we believe. Our lives change when our beliefs change. Sometimes we equate a belief with an opinion, but belief is far more than that. Belief is an active condition, and it results in action. We have many beliefs. Not all of them are religious.

Some years ago, in a country where Americans were not favored, I noticed a young man on a motorcycle across an intersection from us. Something in his behavior caused me to believe that he intended to run us down. As the light changed and we started to cross the street, he gave the motorcycle full throttle and headed it directly toward us. Having anticipated that he intended to do this, I was able to dodge the impact and to pull my wife out of his path. The belief that we were at risk was not a passive thing. It was an active poising to respond, which I felt in every nerve and muscle of my body.

Believing in Christ is not a response of fear. But it is as fully an active poising to respond as was my belief that I was in danger. Belief in Christ is a poising of our whole being to know God as revealed in Jesus Christ and to participate without hindrance in the Kingdom, which involves receiving the full flow of God's love in every facet of our existence. God's openness to being known by us, this opportunity to participate in the Kingdom, and this free-flowing gift of God's love are not "timed" exposures. They are eternal. This is our experiencing of eternal life. Any termination of our relationship with God, any limitations or obstructions that exist, are brought by us into this relationship. God sets no such limitations.

What must we do in return for God's gift of love? Our reaction to God's love is not a transaction—not a business dealing. What we do is a voluntary response. When we love deeply, we want to give. What can mortal humans give to God? Jesus will do his will. They will obey his words, not grudgingly, but gratefully.

We can also share with others what has been shared with us. For two thousand years Christians have been sharing with others the good news of the love and the relationship that God is eager to offer. We can refuse this offered love and relationship, but the offer remains open to all.

Movie- passion

Heaven
Sky
earth
Sheol
Relm of the Dead

21
Do Not Let Your Hearts Be Troubled

John 14

Do not let your hearts be troubled. Believe in God, believe also in me. In my Father's house there are many dwelling places. If it were not so, would I have told you that I go to prepare a place for you? And if I go and prepare a place for you, I will come again and will take you to myself, so that where I am, there you may be also. And you know the way to the place where I am going.   John 14:1-4

WORDS FOR BIBLE TIMES

The time had almost come. Jesus knew that soon they would kill him. But he still had so much that he needed to teach. He had tried to prepare his disciples for the approaching trauma. They sensed that he was preparing to leave them, but they could not understand why. They had begun to protest. Why couldn't they go with him? They could, he assured them, but first he had to go to prepare a place for them, and they knew the way.

Jesus' words must have confused the disciples. So Thomas asked, "Lord, we do not know where you are going. How can we know the way?" (John 14:5).

One natural assumption the disciples may have had was that Jesus was going to the Temple in Jerusalem. The Temple was considered to be God's house. And certainly all the disciples knew the way to the Temple.

But Thomas was more perceptive. He sensed that this was not what Jesus meant. So he probed further.

Jesus' response was that he was going to return to his heavenly Father. The disciples at that point seem baffled. They seem to be asking who, what, and where is the heavenly Father? And what is the way to the heavenly Father? Jesus' words were apparently a response to such questions. But Jesus' answer was probably as confusing to the disciples as his initial statement had been.

With Jesus at the peak of his career and with increasing numbers of people coming to hear him, the disciples would hardly be thinking that Jesus would soon die. They were expecting the kingdom of God to burst in upon the scene, abolishing Roman rule and restoring an energized kingdom like David's under God's rule.

Even if the disciples had realized Jesus was speaking of his approach-

*forgiven
unconditional
who they were*

ing death and of his expectation of a heavenly kingdom opening to them, they would most likely have had trouble visualizing these events. From our vantage point in history it is easier to understand what Jesus was trying to tell the disciples than it seems to have been for them. They had not had experiences of the kind he was describing.

Some Jews believed in a general resurrection at the time of God's judgment. A few accepted the Greek notion of Hades as a dry, dusty storage place for the spirits of the departed. But most people with a Jewish background would have been at a loss to know what Jesus meant. They had no doctrine of a life after death.

In all likelihood, these words of Jesus, full of meaning to later generations of Christians, were puzzling to the people who first heard them. However, by the time the Gospel of John was written, Christians facing martyrdom regarded Jesus' words as cherished promises. The hope of eternal life with Jesus Christ and God was the only hope they had. Suffering and death were the certainties they faced in this life. To remain true to their faith, they needed all the help they could get. Surely these words in the Gospel of John, along with other scriptural assurances, did much to enable Christians to remain faithful when they faced persecution.

WORDS FOR OUR TIME

To estimate the number of persons who have found comfort in the passage of Scripture we are studying would be impossible. These verses contain a message of hope that people cling to in times of bereavement.

Jesus' statements give hope to the bereaved that the loss of their loved one is not a loss forever—not the blotting out of a life that is precious to them. Jesus' words are an assurance that the grave is not the end. The bereaved receive comfort from knowing that their loved one is with Christ in God's eternal realm.

Beyond the comfort that Jesus' words give to the bereaved and to those facing death, there are other significant points we need to ponder.

The word *love* receives special emphasis in this chapter. Repeatedly, Jesus makes clear that the evidence of our love is obeying his commandments (John 14:15, 21, 23-24). As important as the arousal of our emotions may be, Jesus emphasized that action is required of those who profess love. The actions he identified as expressions of love are quite specific. We are to feed the hungry, to comfort the sorrowing, to clothe the naked, to visit the lonely. Indeed, we are to imagine ourselves in the place of the needy and the unfortunate and to do what we can to make their lives more tolerable and more fulfilling (Matthew 25:34-40). We need to learn that this is what love "looks like."

Jesus emphasized that he is in God and God is in him and that we are in him as he is in God (John 14:10, 11, 20). The result of this fact, as Jesus points out, is that to have seen one is to have seen the other (John 14:7, 9). When we think seriously about these statements, we may realize that we who believe we are in Christ should be so much like Jesus that to have seen us is to have seen him. Furthermore, we may realize that the church, called the body of Christ (1 Corinthians 12:27), should be so much like Jesus Christ that to see the church is to see him. We have a long way to go before either we or the church are clear reflections of our Lord.

WORDS FOR MY LIFE

The demands that Jesus makes on us are so total, so complete, that they seem almost frightening. *I really hadn't meant to go quite that far,* I find myself thinking. *I'm not the all-or-nothing type. I'm interested in many things. I don't allow any one thing to consume all my time, all my attention. Let's find some sort of a balance here. I hadn't planned for following Christ to be the only thing in my life.*

But Jesus meant what he said. Allegiance to Christ is not just a social game. It is not child's play. This is real. This is "for keeps." No one is forcing me, but there is no middle ground between God's realm and the ways of the world. I cannot live in a private world and commute to God's realm only when I prefer to do so.

Fortunately, I am promised that I will not be left alone (John 14:16-17, 26). I am assured that the Advocate, the Spirit of Truth, the Holy Spirit, will be with me to teach me all things and to remind me of all that Jesus said. Generations of Christians have spoken with profound gratitude of the Companion who supports those who love and serve in obedience to Jesus Christ's commands.

In addition, we have the promise of peace. This peace is not the kind of peace that the world gives: not the cessation of hostilities between nations, nor the tranquility that comes from having money in the bank, not the absence of problems or tensions. No, this is the peace that comes from knowing that God is fully in control and that I am fully within God's love and care—not just for the moment, but eternally. What a tremendous gift!

As I read and ponder the powerful words of Jesus recorded in the Gospel of John, I come to the realization that I can "know the way" (John 14:4), I must decide. I cannot delegate this responsibility to someone else. Nobody can do it for me. I must obey the commandments. I must do my part in establishing and maintaining the relationship. But I will receive help from an Advocate who will stay with me forever (John 14:16, 26).

22
THE SPIRIT HELPS US

Romans 8

The Spirit helps us in our weakness; for we do not know how to pray as we ought, but that very Spirit intercedes with sighs too deep for words.　　　Romans 8:26

WORDS FOR BIBLE TIMES

Paul felt confident and secure. The churches he had established were thriving. He had completed the collection of funds for the needy Christians in Jerusalem. *This generous contribution should silence my critics,* he must have thought as he enjoyed a visit with friends in Corinth.

Having completed the pioneering work in Asia Minor, Paul was ready to leave that work for others to develop. He was now planning a major new undertaking in Rome. He was writing to the church there. He had never been to Rome, but he had heard that there were already many Christians in the city. And Rome was the center from which one could reach every part of the Roman Empire.

If the church at Rome would allow Paul to work from there as his "home base," he could take the gospel to all the rest of the world. His letter would let the church at Rome know who he was and what his message was. He hoped these Christians would approve of him and support him in taking the good news to the whole empire. After he delivered the offering for the needy in Jerusalem, he would go to Rome. Then, with the help of the church there, he could go all the way to Spain. After that the other parts of the empire would be arenas for his work.

The letter Paul wrote to the church at Rome reflected his mature thought. He was at the peak of his career. The letter was thorough, comprehensive, and well-organized. The Roman Christians received it with appreciation and treasured it. This letter became the first in the collection of Paul's letters preserved in the New Testament.

But Paul's letter to the Romans arrived about two years before he did. And when Paul finally arrived in Rome, it was not as he had planned. He had been arrested in Jerusalem (Acts 21:17-36), where he had gone to deliver the collection for the needy. While on his way to Rome as a prisoner, Paul had been shipwrecked with his captors (Acts 27:1–28:11). The Book of Acts ends with Paul under house arrest in Rome. We do not have a written account of his death, but there is little reason to doubt that the Roman authorities executed him. Words that he had written earlier to the Romans now had to apply to him: Was it true that "neither death, nor life,...nor anything else in all creation" was able to separate him from God's love?

WORDS FOR OUR TIME

In Romans 8, Paul described two styles of life. He set them in contrast with each other and made clear which one he had chosen. These two lifestyles are still alternatives open to persons in our time.

Paul characterized one style of life, quite common in our time, as "the flesh." Basically, he referred to living for sensory enjoyment and fulfillment. The sense of sight is gratified with interesting forms and beautiful colors. The sense of smell is captivated with delightful fragrances. The sense of hearing is excited by thrilling sounds. Even the sense of pride is fed with flattery. The initiating and guiding force behind everything one does is the desire to experience pleasure and heightened sensory enjoyment.

Paul maintains that everything in such a style of living is trivial in significance and fleeting in duration. This lifestyle is degrading to human existence, he says, and invariably leads to death.

Paul recommends instead the spiritual life. In this style of life, the indwelling Spirit of God initiates loving relationships, ennobling attitudes and values, significant goals, and enduring accomplishments. In everything, Paul assures us, the Spirit is available to guide our thoughts, actions, and feelings in accordance with the will and purposes of God. The outcome is that we are justified by God, adopted into the family of God as God's children and heirs, and can look forward to glorification with Christ. Such a style of life makes us capable of transforming evil into good through the power of God's love, present in us through Christ.

Paul says that when we follow the spiritual lifestyle, we can be more than conquerors. Not only do we find that the power of God's love can overcome even the worst experiences but that we can derive good from dealing with a bad situation. From defeat we can learn humility. From suffering we can learn patience. The tragedies that threaten us are not only overcome, they are made to enrich and to ennoble our lives.

In our time we can benefit from Paul's insights. His descriptions of the spiritual life were rooted in his own experiences and observations. And his life was one of risks, challenges, hardships, suffering, and commitment. There was nothing frail or insulated about the life Paul led. He was involved and active. Paul's approach to life is as appropriate for our time in history as it was for his. Paul does not give us a set of negative rules or tell us that we should or can avoid encounters with evil. Instead, Paul tells us that we can confront problems, temptations, and negative influences and conquer them by the power of God's love.

WORDS FOR MY LIFE

Paul proclaimed that nothing can separate us from the love of God in Christ. Unfortunately, we often live in such a way that we are unaware of that love. We do things that keep us from experiencing it.

We become so concerned with ourselves that thoughts of God's love are crowded out. We worry about so many things. Our egos are so tender that we devote all our attention and energy to protecting them from getting hurt. We want so many things from life that we exhaust ourselves in struggling to get them. As a result, we push aside opportunities for God's love to enter our lives.

Excessive concern about money can close a life to the entry of God's Spirit. The constant need for money to buy food or clothing or shelter or medical care or other necessities can keep a person scrambling for dollars day and night. And the seemingly continuous rise in prices means that what was enough yesterday is not enough for today or for tomorrow.

Even the work in which we are involved can become a barrier that prevents God's love from entering our lives. Our driving ambitions, the fierce competition for advancement, the fear of alienating anyone who could wreck our career, and anxieties about future security in the job can consume all our waking hours. We can become so engrossed in our work that we do not even consider the possibility of God's love entering our lives.

These concerns may not seem evil to us. Yet they can keep us from living a spiritual life. Notice Romans 8:26-27. We are not left alone to find a way to break loose, to be able to choose what is good.

The Holy Spirit takes the initiative. Especially in the church, the gathered community of believers, the presence of the Spirit brings us the ability to see God at work both in ordinary times and in times of crisis. Romans 8:28 promises that whatever problems may confront us, God comes into our shattered world, working with us to bring good out of evil. Whether we face poverty or terrorism or pain or grief or our own death, we have the chance to conquer—yes, to be more than conquerors—as we allow God's unmeasurable love to be poured into our lives.

23
LOVE, THE MORE EXCELLENT WAY

April 12
7 am
service

1 Corinthians 13

And now faith, hope, and love abide, these three; and the greatest of these is love.

1 Corinthians 13:13

WORDS FOR BIBLE TIMES

A natural harbor brought the ships of the Mediterranean world to the very edge of the ancient city of Corinth. Small shops lined the main street on both sides as it swept up the small hill toward the fortress at its top. In these shops were the items that seafaring men might want. Amply represented in this array were shops where "love" was for sale. It was widely known that sexual desires could easily be satisfied in Corinth.

Corinth also had shrines and temples where pleas for safekeeping and where sacrifices to various gods could be made. Large images of specific gods could be worshiped at conveniently located shrines, and small images suitable for carrying on a journey were offered for sale.

The inhabitants of this city were the people from among whom Paul had organized the church at Corinth. He was quite proud of this congregation. But there were problems.

Persons are influenced by their yesterdays and by their neighbors. And when persons change, seldom do they get rid of all past influences and practices. Most Corinthians regarded the sale of "love" and the worship of idols as legitimate enterprises. In a city where the demand was so constant, it would be surprising if some church members were not involved in some way in these businesses.

Sl[c] by Rom[

As the founding pastor of this congregation, Paul wrote with frankness and gentleness. He sought to encourage and strengthen what was good in these new Christians. Nevertheless, despite Paul's special feelings toward the Christians at Corinth, he was not blind to their defects.

Paul pointed out a dozen or more serious problems. There was dissension within the congregation. Some members were guilty of immorality, competition for honor, misinterpretations of spiritual gifts, and a lack of consideration for one another. Paul urged the Corinthian Christians to correct these problems. And he offered specific guidance.

Underlying the specific problems, however, Paul saw the source of much of the church's difficulty. This larger problem was the lack of genuine Christian love. To counteract and overcome the church's problems, Paul

M

proposed what he called a "more excellent way" (1 Corinthians 12:31). It was a way of love, which he outlined in Chapter 13 of his first letter to the church at Corinth. Generation after generation of Christians have cherished this classic description of love from a Christian perspective.

WORDS FOR OUR TIME

Love is one of the major themes around which entertainment is developed in America. It is almost impossible to see a play, attend a movie, watch a television program, play a videocassette, or listen to radio music without intensive exposure to the "love theme" in a rather explicit form. But the level of understanding seems far removed from the love Paul describes in 1 Corinthians 13. "Making love" is portrayed as little more than mutual consent in the act of sexual intercourse. And sexual gratification seems to be regarded as the fulfillment of the human need for love. How pathetically naive!

Paul wrote of mutual care, of concern for persons on a continuing basis. Such love, he realized, contributes to the elimination of all sorts of problems and enriches the lives of all people. Such love is profoundly needed in our time. Paul knew that spiritual gifts are affected by the presence or absence of Christian love. Various publicized expressions of "true" Christianity today need to be evaluated by Paul's understanding of Christian love.

Love that dominates and uses the other person for our own satisfaction produces mutually degrading relationships. Current portrayals of love frequently show persons using one another as they would a spoon or a wrench or a bath towel or any other object, not as the thinking, feeling, sensitive human being that the other person actually is. Undoubtedly, the prevailing understanding of one's spouse as a tool for self-gratification has contributed to the high rate of divorce in our society. We throw away objects that have become obsolete or that do not work as well as they did when they were new.

How can Christians encourage enduring relationships rooted in genuine love? How can we resist the tendency to "play it cool" through impersonal liaisons, "one-night stands," multiple relationships, and the mastery of techniques? It is little wonder that our time is characterized as an era of personal loneliness lived in the midst of crowds.

Without knowing what love really is, we are not able to establish the mutually enriching and ennobling relationships that we need. Instead, we tend to see a mass of impersonal, unfeeling, unconcerned objects moving around us and touching us. Paul's guidance in recognizing and seeking authentic love offers a much-needed corrective to the understanding of the so-called "good life" in our time.

WORDS FOR MY LIFE

Fortunately, we do not have to be limited to the understandings the entertainment media provide. We can draw on Paul's insights to help see how to live with one another as Christians.

Occasionally we will need to step back from our routines and activities and take a careful look at ourselves and our relationships. If I continue as I am, what words or phrases would characterize my existence? Am I a user of other people, a human parasite? Or am I a contributor, giving to others at least as much as I take from them? Is my life mostly cooperation, helping others develop to their highest potential? Or is it mostly competition, trying always to outdo those around me? Is this what I really want my life to be? Or is there a more excellent way to live?

Paul has suggested that three things are enduring: faith, hope, and love. Love, he says, is the greatest of these. Would any of these virtues characterize my life? Would those who know me best describe me as a person of faith? Do others think of me as a hopeful person? Do I resemble in any way the description of one whose life exemplifies love?

If not, what is lacking? Am I without patience or kindness? Am I jealous? boastful? arrogant? rude? Do I insist on having my own way even at the expense of other people? Do I become irritable or resentful when things do not go my way? Am I glad to be able to say "I told you so" when things go wrong? Or do I enjoy seeing what is right win out?

We can evaluate our development as Christians by these criteria, which Paul has provided. Where we see our life reflecting tendencies quite different from those Paul listed, we can see where we need to put our efforts to make life better for ourselves and for others.

Persons who have experienced authentic love, such as that which Paul describes, know that the best, most richly meaningful, most desirable aspects of one's being will open up and thrive in its presence, as a flower does in the warm sunlight. When genuine love is present, the full opening of one life to another life occurs. What is finest in each person is tenderly nurtured. Neither person feels any threat of destruction or denigration by the other. The persons involved see clearly that such a relationship is mutually enriching and ennobling. It is in this relationship of authentic love that we are meant to grow and function as human beings.

The shocking contrast between authentic love and the war, exploitation, hatred, and insensitivity that dominate our world shows us how far astray we have gone. With Paul's guidance perhaps we can move again toward more humane forms of existence and relationships on our planet.

24
NEW CREATION IN CHRIST

2 Corinthians 5:14-21

If anyone is in Christ, there is a new creation: everything old has passed away; see, everything has become new! All this is from God, who reconciled us to himself through Christ, and has given us the ministry of reconciliation.

2 Corinthians 5:17-18

WORDS FOR BIBLE TIMES

"Happy New Year!" we tell one another annually. The apostle Paul long ago had an even more exciting phrase. To the Corinthian Christians he felt like saying, "Happy New Creation!"

Paul proclaimed that a new era was in the midst of being born. Sin and death had been condemned and were on their way to oblivion. No longer would people be tempted by sin. No longer would death be the end of every life. Even in the world of nature the effects would be clear. Neither death nor decay would exist among plants and animals.

This was Paul's belief. It was at the heart of his message and of his work. For him, the old era was gone. The new era would be different. It would be without sin, without death, without decay, without evil. Only God's children would be brought into this new world—only those who were reconciled to God through Christ, only those into whose lives God's love had been poured through the Spirit of Christ, only those in whom God's Spirit was dwelling, only those who were in Christ, only those who were God's heirs, with Christ as the first-born.

A belief in a new era was acceptable in the Gentile world. One view of history was different from every other age. So the notion that a new era was being born and the old era was passing away was no problem for the Gentiles.

Many Jews were also ready to hear Paul's ideas. Jewish apocalyptic literature (literature that dealt with the "last days" and the end of time) predicted the end of this world and a final judgment. Some of this literature foretold the appearance of a new and perfect era in place of the old world order. Although there is little evidence that familiarity with this apocalyptic literature caused Jews to accept Paul's preaching, being aware of these writings did make his ideas seem a bit less strange to them.

The effect of Paul's preaching was to motivate both Gentiles and Jews to seek reconciliation with God through Christ. Many people wanted to be included in the new era. They did not want to be sent into oblivion as part of the old era God had condemned. The persecutions of Christians that soon began were made more tolerable because believers thought of these persecutions as the temporary final struggles of sin, evil, Satan, and death. The new creation would be a joy to see.

WORDS FOR OUR TIME

The complex character of our society may contribute to a misunderstanding of what it means to be a Christian. The number of organizations, movements, and coalitions we are urged to join and support is almost beyond comprehension. Our political preference may lead to membership in a specific political party—with a membership card to affirm that relationship. The occupation we choose to pursue may lead us to membership in an organization composed of persons who do the same kind of work—with a membership card affirming that relationship. So, we should not be surprised that occasionally people speak and act as if being a Christian is simply another personal preference resulting in membership in an organization and the receipt of a membership card.

Paul's statements provide a needed corrective to such a misunderstanding. Paul makes clear that being a Christian involves at least three major changes: (1) one is reconciled to God; (2) the love of God is poured into one's life through Christ; and (3) one becomes a new creature. This process is considerably different from joining a club or contributing to a cause or supporting a specific group.

Another reminder that we need in our time is the insight that being a Christian is a serious responsibility. We find it is easy to slip into the routine many members of large organizations have: pay the dues, attend the meetings, support the leadership, and perform specific duties when asked to do so.

Paul clearly affirms that being a Christian is far more demanding. To each Christian and to each group of Christians, God has entrusted the ministry of reconciliation. Each Christian is an ambassador for Christ. Christians are God's means of appealing to those who are alienated. An important fact to note is that God is not alienated from humankind. God wants and actively seeks a reconciliation. It is we who are alienated from God. We reject the love of God that should be filling our lives. Christians have the responsibility to persuade people to accept that love and to allow themselves to be reconciled to God.

WORDS FOR MY LIFE

Since God is seeking reconciliation with each of us, what is preventing it (that is, in those who are not reconciled)? And here the issue can become a bit "touchy." In whose opinion and by what criteria do we judge whether we (or others) are in need of reconciliation or whether reconciliation has already taken place? In Paul's view it is a simple matter. If one is "Spirit-filled," one is a Christian and has been reconciled to God. If one is not "Spirit-filled," one is not a Christian and has not been reconciled to God. And by "Spirit-filled," Paul means that one's life is filled with God's love, a love that is evident in every action and relationship. All one's thoughts and actions are focused on doing God's will and seeking to accomplish God's purposes.

I do not find Paul's test easy to apply. The results are hard to interpret. In most cases those who are called Christians raise no question in my mind. Their lives reflect the virtues, the attitudes, and the behavior patterns that Jesus taught. But now and then there are exceptions. Some of the most generous, conscientious, joyous, caring persons I know are not Christians. And some of the most difficult people to be around—persons who are narrow-minded, mean-spirited, and self-centered—are rigidly "religious." They are very much at home with the vocabulary of the gospel and are familiar with and devoted to the Scriptures. On which persons should my efforts be focused in terms of urging reconciliation with God?

Paul was a dramatically different person after his conversion. But in the case of most people, the new creation they become is not markedly different from the person they were, especially after the experience of change has had time to wear off a bit.

Perhaps we cannot make accurate judgments about our fellow human beings. Perhaps I am wrong to spend my time and energy trying to determine whether another person needs reconciliation. If the new creation is so evident in my life that its benefits over the self-serving life make it attractive and something to be desired, opportunities will be opened to attempt a ministry of reconciliation with those who need and want reconciliation.

However, we need to avoid deluding ourselves. The other person may not be the one who is most in need of reconciliation with God. Perhaps we are the ones who need it. Perhaps I need to begin with myself and ask: *Do my thoughts and actions express the fullness of God's love, or do my own selfish desires control my thoughts and actions?* Perhaps it is our lives into which God is yearning to pour love.

25
GOD IS LOVE

1 John 4:7-12

Beloved, let us love one another, because love is from God; everyone who loves is born of God and knows God. Whoever does not love does not know God, for God is love.

1 John 4:7-8

WORDS FOR BIBLE TIMES

A God of power was very important in the long history of the Israelites. God's invincible might had brought them from their lowly beginnings as nomadic herdsmen to become, by the time of David and Solomon, one of the dominant powers of the eastern Mediterranean lands. God's power brought the Exile when Israel went astray, but God's power led the people back to rebuild Jerusalem. The Hebrews watched other great empires brought down by the power of God's judgment upon them. So they waited confidently for the crushing of mighty Rome and the restoration of David's kingdom by a messiah who would make God's power evident.

Jesus brought a different vision. Love, not power, was the foremost attribute of God. The coming Kingdom would reflect God's righteousness, justice, and love. Which view was the one to believe? Some Jews accepted Jesus as the Messiah and became Christians. Others did not. Within a fairly short time the Jews and Christians separated from one another and have continued as distinctly different faiths ever since.

Meanwhile, an aggressive group had arisen within Christianity that was tearing the churches apart. The members of this movement claimed to have a special knowledge revealed to them by Christ and not available to anyone except through them. Some said that Jesus only seemed to be the Christ. Others said that he was not the Christ but only the human being in whose body the Christ dwelt briefly when he taught them the secrets of spirituality and immortality.

A major part of our New Testament is composed of the letters Christian leaders sent in response to the struggles facing the various churches. First John is one of those letters. The writer was, for the most part, gentle in his use of words; but he "lowered the boom" on the dissident group. How, he kept asking his readers, do we decide who has true knowledge of God? Look at people's lives and see how they act in relation to others. Since God is love, those who know God love one another. But those who do not love do not know God.

The writer must have expected Christians of his day to recognize that the dissidents did not know God. They were anything but loving in their approach and actions. They were proud of their "secret knowledge" and condescending toward other believers. They were arrogant in their demands for financial support from the churches and snobbishly exclusive in their membership. They were uncooperative with other church leaders and determined to have their own way without concern for the damage they did to the churches.

John's letter alone was not enough to solve the problem. The struggle went on for generations—even centuries. But eventually the dissident position was declared a heresy, and the understanding that John had outlined was accepted as the correct one.

WORDS FOR OUR TIME

Love is fully evident in the lives of some Christians today. Some congregations give immediate evidence of love for God's children in their midst and elsewhere. Unfortunately, this love is not always apparent. A common complaint by persons visiting church services is, "It was a cold church." No one spoke to them. They were ignored as outsiders. They were avoided as strangers.

Possibly some congregations feel no love toward strangers. Perhaps the members of some congregations are unskilled in approaching persons they do not know. Or it may be that the visitor has attended a service that is quite different from the services in his or her "home" church in either ritual or emphasis. As a result, the visitor fails to experience any feelings of warmth or of "belonging."

Sincere, fully committed Christians can and do differ from one another at many points. Some Christians emphasize getting ready for the end of the world and anticipating the joys of heaven. Others focus on specific actions to apply their faith by fostering justice. Some concentrate on the conversion of the "unsaved." Still others cultivate the inner, personal, devotional life. Others work for personal and public morality.

Some like exuberant expressions of emotion in worship. Others prefer periods of reverent silence for quiet meditation and personal prayer. Some want thunderous denunciations of specific sins. Others want inspiration and help for daily living.

The differences are good and important for Christianity, but they should not reduce the love Christians have for one another. People with similar preferences tend to seek out one another. But this tendency should not lead to alienation from those who have other preferences.

Personal preference should not cause us to forget our need for one another. There are lonely people in our churches. There are persons who are experiencing heartbreaking events in their lives. There are persons whose anxiety level approaches panic as they look at a future they fear. And there are persons who have exhausted their physical and material resources and feel they have nowhere to turn. Such human pain and tragedy need to be surrounded by the love and help of the whole congregation. If we know the love of God and live as God's children, that will be so.

However, many times the needed love and emotional support from fellow Christians are not offered. This neglect may not be intentional. It may be simple thoughtlessness. We live busy lives, somewhat insulated and isolated from one another. But that does not excuse us from our responsibility to express the love we have received from God, especially at times when other persons need loving words, deeds, and relationships.

WORDS FOR MY LIFE

The consciousness that God loves me makes a big difference in my life. This awareness gives me freedom to be the person I really am.

When I believe that someone is watching every move I make in the hope of finding an opportunity to "cut me down," I tend to live defensively. I think twice before I speak or act. I am careful to expose only my ideas or actions that I am sure will be acceptable. I feel constricted, not fully the person I really am.

Then imagine how it would be to believe that an unfriendly God is watching. Doubly disconcerting would be the knowledge that nothing could be hidden from God. To live in the belief that God is not loving but hostile would result in constant misery and inescapable anxiety.

What a difference it makes to believe that God loves me, that God wants a continuing relationship with me, and that I am accepted as God's child. Knowing that God understands me and approves of me as I am, I am free to fill my soul with the beauties and joys of God's creation. I can allow my feelings and relationships to be authentic and open.

With such love and acceptance by God, living as a loving person and relating to others in love does not have to be "worked at." My obligation as a Christian to be a loving person is not a burden. It is the natural result of my acceptance of God's gift of love.

Regrettably we all know persons who are rather hard to love. We must remember that God loves them. God loves us too, even though we as human beings share responsibility for the death of his Son. "Since God loved us so much, we also ought to love one another" (1 John 4:11).

26
A NEW HEAVEN AND A NEW EARTH

Revelation 21:1-6

Then I saw a new heaven and a new earth; for the first heaven and the first earth had passed away. . . . And the one who was seated on the throne said, "See, I am making all things new." Revelation 21:1, 5

WORDS FOR BIBLE TIMES

"You are a Christian!" At times during the early decades of the church, this simple accusation was sufficient cause for arrest and trial. Unless the accused Christian was willing to curse Christ, deny being a Christian, and demonstrate patriotism by worshiping an image of the Roman emperor, the death penalty could result. Often the executions were in public arenas. The most terrifying procedures imaginable were used—unleashing wild animals to kill and eat the condemned Christians, burning them alive, and tearing their bodies apart limb from limb. The authorities wanted the horror of the executions to dissuade persons from becoming Christians. Accused Christians were usually given three chances to renounce their faith during the course of their trial.

Even prominent leaders such as Peter and Paul suffered execution for the "crime" of being Christians. And the persecutions were continuing. No improvement in this situation seemed likely.

Some persons regarded this discouraging set of circumstances as confirmation of their understanding of cosmic history. They taught that perfection, a true golden age, occurred at the beginning of the world. But from that time on, things got worse and worse through successive periods or ages. Christians were led to believe that things would continue to get ever worse and that eventually all world order would collapse, and the earth would be destroyed.

How reassuring it must have been to hear or read another view, proclaiming another vision of the future: "Then I saw a new heaven and a new earth; for the first heaven and the first earth had passed away, and the sea was no more" (Revelation 21:1).

Best of all, this new beginning was to be provided by God, who had created everything initially. No longer were the Christian's hopes dependent on a change of heart in the Roman emperor or on the compassionate silence of potential informers. With everything swept clean, the new creation was to be God's fresh gift. The opportunity to start all over in a new and perfect creation must have been exciting to contemplate.

Until this new heaven and new earth came, what was required of Christians? To hold fast and continue in the faith was their task. And this they were already doing in the face of persecution and possible death from the Roman authorities. Now Christians had additional hope.

The message of the Book of Revelation was a new promise and a most encouraging word to Christians. This book told them that they would be victorious whether they lived or died. If they died as Christian martyrs, they would receive immediate entrance into heaven and an honored status there. If they lived as Christians, they would soon see the new heaven and the new earth appear for their eternal enjoyment. Christians found new courage in the vision.

WORDS FOR OUR TIME

Discouragement is a problem for Christians in our time just as it was for Christians in the early days of the church. Like those first believers, we see no evidence of God's just and righteous kingdom being established on our planet. Evil influences seem to multiply despite our vigorous efforts to eliminate them. Drug abuse, child abuse, the corruption of trusted officials, acts of terrorism, warfare, theft, "white collar" crimes, and a multitude of other evils seem out of control and beyond our ability to combat. As our hopes fade, our apathy tends to increase and our Christian activity begins to decline.

"I have a dream," proclaimed Martin Luther King, Jr., a generation ago. For many people, his dream was a vision of the new heaven and new earth. He spoke of peace, justice, and opportunity for everyone under the rule of God.

The dream of such a world releases power in us to work for it, provided that we believe it is a live possibility—a realistic option. But many people grow weary after striving for ideals that often seem beyond their reach. They feel that they have expended their energies futilely. Promises by political leaders frequently turn out to be nothing more than empty phrases. Calls to heroic action by our religious leaders have produced few enduring gains. So, despite significant investments of our energies and our resources, we always seem to remain about where we began.

Perhaps the time has come to ask what help we can expect beyond our own efforts as we try to be Jesus Christ's authentic followers. Is there a power beyond the superpowers of the world, a force mightier than the nuclear forces stockpiled for our destruction? Certainly our faith is rooted in the confidence that there is such a power, such a force. God is our loving parent.

Can we articulate our belief in the help that goes beyond our human resources? Can we express it so all can have a realistic expectation to which they can give their support? That seems to be our challenge and our task.

WORDS FOR MY LIFE

We must be careful to avoid being unrealistic. Persons involved in science and technology may exaggerate human abilities. Because science, medicine, and communication have come so far in recent years, some people begin to think there is no limit to what human beings can do. We may forget that we are not the creators of our own existence.

The vision from the Book of Revelation and the memory of how Christians of that period were persecuted remind us that it is God, not we, from whom all creation comes. We need to recall the futility of repeated human efforts and the tragedy of repeated human failures. Human attempts do not bring the world we desire. Our awareness must be, as that of our spiritual ancestors has been, that the God we worship is the God of history, shaping and forming the destiny of us all.

Instead of despair at the failures of our leaders, the vision from Revelation can give us courage. God, who is continuously making all things new (Revelation 21:5), has brought us this far. Our imperfect world, with all its deplorable defects, would have seemed like the answer to prayer if it had arrived to replace the world the early Christians endured.

Most of us have trouble being patient, but we need to take time to see where God is leading. What futures are being opened to us in these days?

Amidst all the chaos and turmoil of our times, God is bringing into being a new creation. But there are demands on each of us if we are to enter this new world and to participate in its benefits. There is no place for my old provincial prejudices or for my deeply ingrained selfishness. Instead, I am being asked to join the family of God, where justice, self-respect, righteousness for all, and full opportunity for everyone are required.

All this demands that I deeply and sincerely search for the will of God in every situation. I need to search for this as vigorously and as tirelessly as humankind searches for cures for our most dreaded diseases. I need to search for this as patiently as scientists search the limits of outer space for signs of other life forms. I need to search until I find God's purpose for me today and always.